COMPARATIVE PSYCHOLOGY

AND

UNIVERSAL ANALOGY.

VOL. I.

VEGETABLE PORTRAITS OF CHARACTER,

COMPILED FROM VARIOUS SOURCES, WITH ORIGINAL ADDITIONS.

BY

M. EDGEWORTH LAZARUS, M.D.

"There is no great and no small
To the *Soul* which maketh all,
For where it cometh all things are,
And it cometh every where."—R. W. Emerson.

Every hidden science is but a letter detached from the name of Jehovah.
Alphonse Constant.

NEW YORK:
FOWLERS & WELLS, PUBLISHERS,
CLINTON HALL, 131 NASSAU STREET.
1851.

To
Mary Ellen M......
The Orange Flower of Mobile,
THIS LITTLE BOOK IS DEDICATED
as a homage of Affection

INDEX.—VOL. I.

PRELUDE OF MOTTOES.

GIVE me of the Vine
Whose ample leaves and tendrils curled
Among the silver hills of heaven,
Draw everlasting dew;
Wine of wine,
Blood of the world,
Form of forms, and mould of statures,
That I intoxicated,
And by the draught assimilated,
May float at pleasure through all natures;
The bird-language rightly spell,
And that which roses say so well.

* * * * * * *

Come learn with me the fatal song
Which knits the world in music strong,
Whereto every bosom dances,
Kindled with courageous fancies.
Come lift thine eyes to lofty rhymes,
Of things with things, of times with times,
Primal chimes of Sun and shade,
Of sound and echo, man and maid,
The land reflected in the flood,
Body with shadow still pursued.
For Nature beats in perfect tune,
And rounds with rhyme her every rune,
Whether she work in land or sea,
Or hide underground her alchemy.
Thou canst not wave thy staff in air,
Or dip thy paddle in the lake,
But it carves the bow of beauty there,
And the ripples in rhymes the oar forsake.

RALPH WALDO EMERSON.

PREFACE.

ALLEGORICAL PORTRAITS OF NATURE;

OR,

VEGETABLE AND ANIMAL CHARACTERS.

HUMAN portraitures are here illustrated by the flower, bird, beast, or insect, in which the pencil of the Divine artist has traced upon the canvas of nature the animate symbols of passions and characters.

Grandville, in his fascinating toilet of the "Flowers Personified," has shown how rich a field here opens to us. His work wears, however, only the evanescent charm of a freak of fancy; this has a higher claim, whose appreciation we trust to you. Yet it was not amid the cold and colorless heights of abstract science that the delicate buds we now offer you, have been culled. A heart whose pulses throbbed in unison with nature's,—a religious imagination to which flower and bird, and beast and creeping thing were living words of God, have opened her temple and unrolled her scriptures. It was amid warm life where nature poured her soul in odors, colors, forms, and sounds, that these inspirations were born, and it is with such suggestions, and in such environment, that they should be uttered to you. The key of nature's mysteries lies in a pure life and a loving heart; only as we thus bring peace and joy within us, are we open to the inflowing of the universal life; while as sin, disorder, disease, obscure the crystalline lens of the soul, nature's most delicate beauty shows all a blur, and her most musical voices fall unheeded on our ear.

> " Nature wears the color of the spirit,
> Sweetly to her worshipper she sings;
> All the glow, the grace she doth inherit,
> Round her trusting child she fondly flings."

Let us, if possible, escape from cities, from the social maelstroms and treadmills of civilized industry, where human beings are ground up into fabrics, books, papers ; where " things are in the saddle, and ride mankind." The laborer is greater than his work. The healthy indifference and conservatism of all creatures yet happily within the circle of natural instincts, teach us to honor God in ourselves, like the flowers, " whose beauty is their own excuse for being ;" inspires that *faith*, by whose *organic force* the mustard seed, " which is indeed the least of seeds, when it is cast into the ground, grows, and waxes a great tree," as the earth-life freely permeates its tissues.

We shall know that we are healed when calm and unreproved we can press our cheek to our mother earth's great breast, and feel our heart answer to the pulses of her life, as it leaps in the deer, warbles in the bird, glides in the stream, and trembles in the consciousness of its own exquisite animation, through every breeze-kissed flower, and every leaf of the forest harp.

Then—ah, then, in the harmony of life, ceases that void in our being, that fearful poverty which gold cannot remove, to escape from which we struggle through false labors and false pleasures, groping among shadows, like unburied ghosts that wandered on the banks of the ancient Styx ; clutching like Tantalus at the fruit which the wind still swings beyond our reach ; toiling like Sisyphus the self-perfectioneer-er, to roll up the hill of character the stone of his own vices, still destined to fall back to the bottom, crushing us beneath its weight ; or chained like Prometheus, the metaphysician, to a rock, where the vulture, gnawing at our bowels, condemn us to eternal *introspection.*

When the heart is awakened to sympathy with nature, the mind will not rest idle or incurious. It is no longer contented to wander along the road-side, or through vast woodland halls, a mystified stranger, knowing neither the reason of its own existence nor of that which surrounds it.

It asks for the science of Universal Analogy.

Hitherto we have suffered the despair of the victims which the Sphinx of old devoured. Œdipus did not kill her, as the fable asserts. Does she not still pelt us with her riddles on every side ? Is not every created thing still calling upon man to name it, and upbraiding him with the loss of that sympathetic instinct which should enable him to penetrate the secret of its being, and its affinities with his own ?

Those who have been thus gifted, in a degree however limited, have been the founders of our arts, the teachers of agriculture, and the physicians of the people ; for nature contains a cure for every ill that flesh is heir to, and satisfaction for all our wants ; and man, as he learns to complete his being in the marriage with hers, grows sound and happy in his mature life, as formerly a healthy and happy babe, he slept cradled in her arms in the paradise of Eden.

The names given by Adam, whether considered as the first individual man or the first society of men, were not surely arbitrary words, such as those by which we designate creatures. Since the confusion of Babel, separation of interests and isolation of the family household have destroyed the harmony of our race and corrupted its languages. It would have been no great matter of record that Adam, in the surprise occasioned by the presentation of a new object, uttered some articulate cry : we conceive it rather to be signified by the Scripture that the articulate sounds uttered by Adam were expressive of the *essential nature* of all the various creatures, into which his heart, strung in unison with all the sphere, penetrated by sympathy.

His names would have expressed the analogical or hieroglyphical characters by which they were related to himself, as embodying some of those passions and faculties resumed and concentrated in his own being, as the archtype of creation.

In the order of Creation, the highest manifestations of life—to which the rest were to be adapted and subordinated —must have been first conceived. An architect about to build, must first conceive an idea of the whole, as if it stood before him. It shall be a palace, a temple, or a cottage. It shall present the Doric, the Ionic, or the Corinthian method. It shall be round, or square, or conical. He decides upon the method of the whole, forming thus a distinct ideal for attainment. He next comes to calculate the width, height, and thickness of each chamber, column, &c., in reference to this whole to which they must be adapted and subordinated. This rude figure may assist us in conceiving, so far as it is possible to us, of the outflow and manifestation of life from its center in God. In whatever ideas we can have of the creation, we must suppose that its author first conceived the plan of a symmetrical whole upon which he would calculate the special type of each character, entering into it as a component; and give it a definite expression, as in the animal and vegetable kingdoms; commencing from the lowest and simplest forms, which would thus be the first in the order of actual creation, he would gradually ascend to the more composite in approaching his ideal, and terminate in man as the archtype or epitome, combining in a symmetrical whole all parts or special types. Assuming for man this place in the earth's visible creation, the inferior creatures must have been calculated as to their characters, in relation to the human ideal,—some special character of which is typed by each of them. The two principles, of adaptation, resulting from contrast or difference; and adaptation, resulting from resemblance or similitude, here meet. Each creature, in which some passional quality is especially depicted, has, to man in this respect, the adaptation of similitude, which renders it a natural hieroglyphic; whilst its difference from other portions of his nature, establishes towards him adaptations of utility, corresponding to those which each part of the same whole bears to other parts, as their complement—having something which they have not. Example:—The dog, whose various species are adapted to man hieroglyphically, as the emblems of the different sorts of friendship, is adapted differently or in relation of use, to his enmities, as the bloodhound; to his fears and his negligence, as the mastiff and other guard-dogs; to his too feeble powers of destruction, as the setter and other game dogs; to his acquisitiveness, as the sheep-dogs; to his vacancy of heart, as the ladies' muff lap-dog. Most of the present animal and vegetable creation are like the Tiger or the Poison Oak, types of vicious developments of character, and their adaptations are inverted, to the injury instead of to the uses of man. This coincides with the present position among mankind of the characters they picture, which are at war with the general welfare of the individual and the society. So long as conflict of interests and passions obtains within man's bosom, and between man and man; so long must external nature abound in maleficent creations. God has done nothing by halves. When we discover, appreciate and realize an order of social combination, converging and harmonizing each man's passions within himself and towards his neighbor, then we may expect the substitution of beneficent creations, as productive of good as the passions they represent, which will tend as strongly to the ends of justice and general well-being, as now in the disorder and conflict of individual and social interests, they tend to rapacity and general discomfiture.

This is even now pictured to the senses in the order, beauty, and harmony of life in a well-managed and highly cultivated farm, when contrasted with the venomous and ferocious characters of life in the swamp or jungle, yet unreclaimed and discordant, or hostile to the life of man. Such pictures reveal to plain common sense the methods by which science and industry, directed in vast social combinations, may conquer the wilds of nature, and make of the whole earth a paradise.

If we may speak of the mistakes of a race, as of those committed by an individual, it was perhaps most fatal that man should have strayed from his first home in the Eden climates before first forming there under the inspiration of natural harmonies, the order of social relations consonant with the affinities of his varied types of character and passion. In those regions of abundance where blighting poverty has never entered, they might have been—may still be—freely recognized. It is there that attractive industry springs from instinct—from the love of the beautiful objects which ensphere us—there that duty and charm are blended, fruit cultures replace the heavy toil of the grain and root crops of the north, and in operating as a true artist, man finds himself the darling child of Earth and Sun. In the fortunate islands which civilized cupidity has not yet ruined in the South Pacific, the happy savage still listens to the song of the sphere, where the deep bass voice of the murmuring ocean mingles with the tenor of the forest and the soprano of the feathered choir ; the passionate breath of flowers gives language to his love ; the cocoa, the bread-fruit, the banana, drop their homage at his feet ; beasts and birds, all innocent or friendly towards him, only await his invitation to cluster round him as auxiliaries in the industry of his beautiful home. His health, senses, instincts, are sound and unbroken by vices, nor betrayed by false religions and philosophies.

Ah, the harmonic characters will yet, from all the countries where they wander and suffer, return to their climate-homes, and become true psychical electroscopes in whose society the harmonies of nature become potentialized in passional accords. And to flowers, our gratitude, our adoration is ever due, because they ever remind us of this destiny. True always to the memory of their Eden home, they traverse the globe with the bee and the song bird, a little before man, and tell the Eden story to every trustful child, until the Eden glory shall fade in the light of a fairer, happier life. Being is the parent of action—Beauty the inspiration of force. Let us read then a leaf from the Bible of Flowers.

NOTE.—The articles which have no other signature have been translated from the French of CHARLES FOURIER, *Unité Universelle, Tome* iii., *Pivot Inverse, and Manuscripts, passim.*

UNITY OF MAN WITH NATURE,

OR

COMPARATIVE PSYCHOLOGY AND UNIVERSAL ANALOGY.

A LESSON FOR THE LADIES.

"INSTRUCTION for the ladies." Ah! and what may be the subject of your dissertations? Some transcendental pedantry on the unity of man with the universe? Psychological and analogical doctrines? Your very title will suffice to put the ladies to flight. This is a hollow dream, they will say, of some pedagogue in the isms and the ologys—some astrologer or ideologist. Let us leave him to his travels over the vast universe. We decline being of the party. If you would entice the ladies to read one of your chapters, you should, in place of transcendental dissertations on the universe, entwine your calculations with the loves, with roses, and with carnations. It is thus that we present science to the fair.

Thanks for your suggestion; we subscribe to these terms. We shall speak here only of the perfume of flowers and the cooing of turtle doves. We aim in a short lesson upon vegetable and animal allegories, to initiate the ladies into the great mystery of the unity of creation, and to enable them to give lessons on the subject to their learned acquaintance, so often foiled in their researches. The ladies will soon be able to explain to them the enigma, and is it not pleasant to learn in the song of a thrush or the opening of a rose-bud, more of this unity than all the academies know? Messrs. Naturalists, you who have recognized in the rose, the emblem of modesty; in the viper, the emblem of calumny; in the mistletoe, the emblem of the parasite; and in the dog, the emblem of friendship; why have you not extended to all created objects this relation of passional analogy? Why have you not, in pursuance of your own precepts, "to proceed from the known to the unknown," presumed that if the rose and the viper are striking emblems of certain effects of passions, that the carnation and the toad should be equally the hieroglyphics of passions, whose system of representation some unknown theory shall unveil for us?

If the dog and the viper are evidently pictures of friendship and of calumny; why should not other animals, as the horse and the ass, portraits of the soldier and the peasant, be likewise emblematic allusions, pictures of characters?

The system of nature would be very vague, very inconsistent! She would have fashioned in some animals and vegetables images of our passions, whilst other animals and plants would be deprived of these symbolical relations, and consequently excluded from unity and analogy with man, with the passional world. This is not so. The analogy is complete in the different kingdoms of nature. In all their details they mirror some effect of our passions.

They form an immense museum of allegorical canvas on which the crimes and the virtues of humanity are painted. The science which is at last to explain these numberless enigmas is Universal Analogy or Comparative Psychology. It is one of the branches of Attraction, which we have disdained, like coffee, during thousands of years. Antiquity more happily inspired, had breathed upon the secret. Drawing nearer to nature, its instinct had perceived, if not penetrated, the secret of analogy between the passions and external creation. Its poets had established an illusion upon every object. In their ignorance of the theory of emblems, they guessed at them in their myths.

There to enchant us fairy spells are playing,
Ideals from the spirit world in fairest forms arraying;
The fleeting types of truth and force are shrined in Deity,
In wise and warlike Pallas, or the wave-born Queen of Beauty.
Echo, no longer tost upon the fitful gusts of air;
Beside some lake, between the hills, now drops her love-drawn tear:
Thus sipping like the humming-bird the dew of fancy's flowers,
The Poet wings his sunny flight, borne on the bridled hours:
His shuttle weaves the cloud's gray fleece in robes of rainbow glory,
And sea and sky, and bird and flower, to him unfold their story.

The ancients had perceived the secret of nature—universal analogy. They started from a true principle, but they knew not how to apply it. Their allegories were fantastic, they lacked the theory of interpretation, the art of explaining methodically the sense of every animal, vegetable, and mineral hieroglyphic. If there are in the productions of nature some striking pictures, such as the horse and the ass, in which we easily recognize the portraits and characters of the soldier and the peasant—other pictures, as those of the bee-hive and the hearts-ease flower, must appear to us quite incomprehensible, for they paint social effects which do not yet exist, and which are reserved for the combinations of the future. Natural history is yet an insipid study, though here and there the eye of some priest or poet of her temple, of Huber, or Audubon, irradiates the dark. In vain may Buffon or Linnæus boast the charm of their labors, they have made only a body without a soul, in presenting them to us unsupported by the allegories which will make us love by their title of portraits, a flower, a fruit, a leaf, a root; because we shall see in them a mirror of our souls, of the play of our passions. Should we be presented with an assorted bouquet of the Iris flower, of which there are several varieties, from the highly fragrant butterfly Iris, to the colossal Iris—gray-spotted, without perfume; the collection would possess but a moderate interest for us, and the less that several species, as the wall Iris and the gray colossal Iris, are of a dull and sad shade, one without perfume, the other of a bitter and disgusting smell. But all become interesting even by their somber tints, when we learn that they offer us the picture of the varieties of marriage, and that they represent exactly its different effects in the different conditions of life :—

Marriage of Young Lovers, . .	Butterfly Iris.
Marriage of Poor Laborers, . .	Wall Iris.
Marriage of Citizen Class, in comfortable circumstances, ...	Blue Iris.
Marriage of Opulent Lovers, . .	Yellow and Azure Iris.
Marriage of Ambition or Princes, .	Gray Colossal Iris.

The details of this analogy, extended to a dozen varieties, will invest with a charm even the most inodorous species, as the wall Iris. Thus, in a museum, the pictures of serpents and monsters become by their truthfulness, as attractive as those of more lovable animals. We turn displeased from the lugubrious aspect of the large Iris spotted with black. It pompously displays the colors of mourning, and we might call it the flower of great mourning, without perfume, without color.

Whence comes this contrast of luxury and sadness? It is needed by the analogy with the conjugal unions of princes, whence the accords of love are excluded, since they marry without having even seen each other. Chance may render such alliances happy, but in principle, they are deprived of the mainspring of conjugal harmony. God must then paint this political servitude by an emblem sadly pompous, as the great gray Iris, a sumptuous flower which he has deprived of perfume as a symbol of those marriages whose tie is simple and charmless, where the accessories of state and grandeur preside, whilst those of love are excluded. The type of the latter exhales in the perfume of the blue, yellow, and butterfly Iris, emblems of marriages happy by the alliance of love with fortune.

This emblem of marriage bears three caterpillars on its three petals. Now whenever the vegetable kingdom represents the caterpillar form, as in the Euphorbia, and the Heliotrope after its flowers are shed, we are to look for a subversive character, some falsehood—some disgrace, something incomplete and latent, the caterpillar being the principal emblem of purgatorial states, and of their metamorphosis into happier orders, typed by the butterfly, which succeeds the venomous and disgusting insect, as order and harmony are to succeed to the abominations of the false societies characterized by the isolated household and the competitive workshop. The Iris furnishes successively two corollas or flowers, which seem to avoid, to isolate themselves from each other. The second, long hidden, suddenly appears when the first withers. This is the image of the conjugal bond which unites a young woman to an old man. The age of pleasure is not common between them. It sets for one and dawns for the other. Thus the second flower only opens when the first is withered. The corolla of the Iris seems to be formed of three distinct flowers artificially united at their stems. Marriage is also a group of three affections, quite distinct, and often painfully connected.

Simple Material Love, ...	Dull Blue.
Conjugal or Domestic Alliance, . . .	False Violet.
League of Family or Paternity, . . .	Yellow.

These three colors correspond to the three passional effects. The receptacle of the stamens, in caterpillar form, types the sordid calculations which preside over marriage. Three accessory petals rise and approach each other, graciously abandoning the body of the flower, whilst the three productive seed-bearing petals isolate themselves and seem to avoid each other. Thus in marriage, the three sexes, man, woman, and child, seek away from each other, and from home, the pleasures of congeniality, so rarely existing in domestic life, where we oftener find discord and restraint. By analogy, nature compresses into a fan the leaf of the common Iris. It depicts the constraint of poor marriages and small households. The leaf of the common Iris is terminated by a dry point, a sign of the poverty in which the work of poor families results. We should say, from the crushing of the leaves at their issue from the root, that they lacked space to extend and unfold themselves.

As there are rich and happy, as well as poor and ill-constituted families, nature has painted this duplicity in the effects of marriage, in giving to the symbolic plant a double formation of its roots and leaves, notwithstanding the unity of arrangement in the flower.

Nature images in her hieroglyphical types of our passions, the customs and characters of the past, present, and future. Until the naturalist takes his point of view from the passions themselves, he can observe only effects without knowing the causes which have regulated their distribution. If we ask them why the lily is covered with a pollen which treacherously soils the face of its gatherer, why the carnation irregularly bursts its calyx, they are forced to retrench themselves in the solemn depths of a decree, and behind the opacity of brazen veils. In other words, they are as blind as moles in calculating causes, limiting their studies to the simple method of classifying effects.

If we are ignorant of the causes which have influenced each detail of creation, we are tempted every moment to complain of nature and its wise author, whose faithful pencil we should admire if we knew how to determine by analogy the meaning of their pictures.

If the lily did not smear our noses, it would be no longer the truthful interpreter of the dangers incurred by him who would practice truth and straightforwardness in civilized society. Have you not been tempted to censure Nature for depriving of fragrance such superb flowers as the tulip, ranunculus, and others? This prejudice will vanish when we come to discuss the inodorous flowers, which appear exceptionable when considered simply in themselves, but not as pictures of our passions and characters.

In these descriptions the analogy must be supported by details upon the forms, colors, habits, properties, of the flower, of the leaves, the seeds, the roots. To this we shall soon return. We are here simply preluding, and limit ourselves first to state the absolute void of research in this field, to publish the shortcomings of science, which establishes no emblematic ties nor relations between the products of nature and our passions; and which, notwithstanding, dins our ears with the unity of the universe, with the universal bond between all parts of the system of nature. Where, then, is the link between plants and passions? To what effect of passion is linked this flower called Iris? To what passion does each of our many thousand plants correspond? The same question to animals and minerals? Thereupon our learned wigs reply, by the impenetrability of deep profundities, and the sacrilegious audacity of that rash reason which would fathom the eternal decrees. Some authors have recognized the vice of our actual methods in the study of nature. Rousseau complains bitterly of those theories, which, as he says, spit Greek and Latin at us, in order to interest us in a plant. The botanist, with his barbarous jargon of tragopogon, mesembryanthemum, tetandria, rhododendron; will disgust you with a science to which the explanation of a social allegory will attract you at once. Let us judge of this by two much slighted plants, the (buis) broom and the mistletoe. Nothing is less interesting than the broom—emblem of poverty. It inhabits barren spots and ungrateful soils, like the poor who is reduced to take up with the most miserable shelter, with some site which every one else disdains. We see insects attach themselves to the broom, as to the poor who lacks the means of cleanliness. Like the wretch who patiently endures privation and puts up with the most paltry lodging, the broom braves the blast and the sleet, and binds itself firmly to the bad soil to which it is exiled. The poor has no pleasures. Nature has painted this effect in depriving the flower of petals, the emblems of pleasure. Its fruit is a pot turned upside down, the image of the kitchen of the poor which is reduced to nothing. Nature paints this effect by upsetting the pot, which in all countries is the foundation of the kitchen. Its leaf is dug out into a spoon to collect a drop of water, like the hand of the poor which seeks from the wayfarer the obolus of compassion. Its wood is very hard, compressed, and knotty, in allusion to the rough life and to the constraint of the wretch steeped in squalid penury, typed by the fetid oil which is drawn from the broom.

The picture of the parasite is not less faithful in the mistletoe, living on the sap juices of another plant; growing indifferently, upward or downward, like the intriguer who takes all masks.

The mistletoe figures duplicity by its leaf, and spreads with its glue the snare in which birds catch themselves, as dupes are caught by the cunning of the parasite. Thus, such objects which at first excite only disdain and criticism, grow beautiful from the fidelity of their pictures and hieroglyphical justice. Without this application, nature appears to us lifeless and simple, devoid of spiritual relation with us, and the Creator seems to be at fault in his wise dispositions. Why, says the critic, not have given fragrance to such superb flowers as the tulip (justice), ranunculus (etiquette), hortensia (coquetry)? We shall see further on, that if these flowers were endowed with fragrance they would be unfaithful paintings; unworthy of the truth which should reign in the pictures of the great artist.

We are continually advised to take counsel from nature. She agrees with us in our contempt for the simple. Like us, she disdains the field flower, and the wild fruit of the forest. She creates them to ally herself with our industry, to adorn and perfect herself by the labors of man, and to yield under his hand, fruits and flowers, not simple, but composite.

It is thus with our studies; they ought to be composite, and not simple. We should investigate in the system of nature, the material and the spiritual, and combine both.

This is something that naturalists have never done. Their methods speak to the eye and not to the soul. They have never sought to link their science with the passions, and to determine the analogy between passions and created objects.

Let us seek in flowers and fruits for lessons addressed to the soul, for emblems of our passions. We begin with the rose, the carnation, and other well-known flowers; thence we shall pass to fruits.

The rose is of all natural pictures that which has been best understood. We can all explain the analogy of the thorn, which lightly wounds the ravisher. Every one sees the emblem of modesty in the bud, which, when but half unfolded, pleases most. The rose, so charming when half closed, is almost slighted when full blown. Thus the young innocent pleases more than the experienced matron, and charms half veiled more than nudities.

The rose presents no difficult allegories. The incarnate glow of its petals well depicts the rosy flush of youth; the plant loves cool spots, symbolic of the freshness of youth, which it images. Its perfume, which we call inaptly the mild perfume of roses, is a most intoxicating aroma, like the love which a truly modest young girl can inspire. In the accessories of this flower there is nothing simple. A highly ornate calyx —a leaf delicately perfumed and indented; all is charming and well cared-for, because the rose does not represent the coarse, simple and rustic shepherdess, but the maiden nurtured in luxury, accustomed to refinement, and heightening the gifts of nature by the assistance of art. Its modesty is not a simple but a composite modesty. This intervention of the labors of art is depicted in the finely indented leaf; the perfume of the leaf types the young girl, who in opulence, is industrious.

THE ROSE.

BY HARRIET WINSLOW.

Maiden, with careless eye,
Pass me not idly by;
Deem me not senseless—soulless, 'tis not so:
With clear and tranquil mind,
With sense far more refined,
I hear the stars sing and the flowers grow.

Low voices greet mine ear,
That mortals may not hear;
Mine their duller sense hath never known:
I hold most sweet discourse
With life's mysterious source,
And yield obedience unto God alone.

Nature reveals to me
Much hidden mystery;
She speaks a language subtle and refined:
Her voices, sweet and clear,
Proud man can never hear;
Audible only to the childlike mind.

The shows of morn and night
Give me far more delight
Than all your costly pleasures can impart:
In higher halls I tread,—
Rich feasts for me are spread,
And robes unrivaled by your boasted art.

I bathe in floods of light,
And from the hand of night
I drink unsparing draughts of crystal dew:
Nor care, nor toil, nor strife
Invade my charmed life;
I wake each morn to rapture ever new.

I know no selfish love;
All pride, all shame above,
My being freely do I offer up:
I taste ethereal bliss
In the sweet zephyr's kiss,
And give back incense from my dewy cup.

Laden with that rich freight,
On mortals he may wait,
And give my fragrant store of sweets away:
Again when he returns,
My heart with rapture burns,
Again I offer all, nor ask repay.

I do not waste my life
With such pure pleasure rife,—
In idle longings for some higher part:

The present is to me
An immortality,
And heaven bends low, and reigns within my heart.

I know, though I am gone,
The rose will still live on;
The soul, the beauty I now body forth,
Immortal and divine,
In other forms than mine,
Will still add glory to the glorious earth.

PASSIONAL ANALYSIS OF PLANTS.

Let us here observe, that in explaining vegetable analogies, each portion of the plant furnishes a generic emblem.

The Root—is the emblem of the principles which regulate the development of passion and character in the class represented.

The Stalk—emblem of the course which the character or passion pursues.

The Leaf—(organ of digestion and respiration)—emblem of the labor of the class or person depicted, and of the labor and care, as those of education, which have prepared a given effect of the passion.

The Calyx—emblem of the forms in which a passion clothes itself; of the surroundings which influence it.

The Petals—emblems of the species of pleasure attached to the exercise of the passion, or to the developed tendencies of the character.

The Pistils and Stamens are the organs and emblems of reproduction and fructification.

The GRAIN—emblem of the treasure acquired by the exercise of the passions, or the results attained by the character or class represented.

The PERFUME—emblem of the charm which the passion excites; of the spiritual atmosphere which the person or class diffuses around it.

These may be abbreviated thus :—ROOT—source; STALK—course ; LEAF—work ; CALYX—clothes ; PETALS—pleasure ; PISTILS and STAMENS—production ; GRAIN—treasure or product attained ; PERFUME—charm.

Why have our skillful commentators on the rose, found in the carnation an impenetrable enigma? Because they lack elementary ideas in this study. They know not yet the analogy of colors, viz. :—violet, friendship ; azure, love ; yellow, paternity; red, ambition ; indigo, emulation or cabalism ; green, alternation or variety ; orange, compositism or enthusiasm of numbers ; white, unitism or sentiment of Deity.

ILLUSTRATIONS.

Without penetrating into essential causes, let us here consider some obvious confirmations of this correspondence of colors with passions.

Just in proportion as the artist appreciates and illustrates the correspondences of passions, colors, sounds, and forms ; does he move us by his music, painting, statue, or edifice. Language affords a very imperfect medium of interpretation.

The passion Ambition has received its principal developments in military life, whose perversions of human nature have absorbed at once the material and passional resources of nations, often scarcely leaving enough to prolong their existence. War has made a gigantic monopoly of glory and heroic energy. Red is the favorite military color, as it is the color of the blood-test by which the questions of ambition are decided. It is the complexion of the sanguine temperament, of which ambition is the dominant passion, though not exclusively so. It excites the belligerent propensities of animals. The Spanish matador waves a red flag before the eyes of the bull to infuriate him. Turkeys, and other creatures, will rush at any red object.

Yellow—Paternity—is the color of the harvest, of ripened seeds and grains in general, is worn by nature in autumn, when like a bountiful parent she "spreads a common feast for all that lives." Plants wear this color then in their season of paternity and fruition, when they have ultimated and expressed their lives in the germs of the future year. They now make their wills and testaments, and bequeath us the wealth they have accumulated through the summer to sustain us through the winter and early spring. Thus the legacy of the patriarch serves for the nurture of a juvenile progeny, and sustains the family through the seasons of inaction and incapacity.

It has been recently discovered that no plant can fructify out of the action of the yellow ray. This fact affirmed *a priori* by passional analogy, remains a property of science like the existence of the Leverrier planet, or of the planets called telescopic, which passional analogy had first announced.

Blue—Love—is the color of the heavens which overarch and encircle the Earth in the embrace of the Sun. The blue tint is an atmospheric effect produced at that point where the influences of these Beings mingle, and where life starts into existence on the surface of the earth as its result. Thus we lose it by ascending out of the limit of the earth's reverberation of the solar ray, as on high mountains or in balloons, where the heavens appear as a dark void above us.

Blue depicts that Love which manifests itself in the contact of the Solar ray, and of the Planet which impregnated by this ray produces all the germs of life from her fertile womb. The color blue is then in correspondence with the individual loves in which this collective planetary love is still farther continually expressed—and this is the more appropriate, because in the mysterious union of the sexes the whole virtue of creation is found mirrored in the object of love, and the love of woman becomes the other pole as it were of the love of God.

In the passional distribution of the planetary scale, Fourier assigns to Herschel the preparation of those aromas whence spring the plants and animals symbolic of Love. "The beauty, the richness and the number of notes (satellites) in the scale of this cardinal of Love, promised to the Earth innumerable series of ravishing, perfumed, delicate, intoxicating types. Cruel deception! No planet has shown itself more sparing of gifts towards its poor sister than the too susceptible cardinal of Love. Herschel has never been able to pardon the earth its moral theories against Love. It is especially in the cast of her vegetable kingdom that this ill-humor breaks forth. Herschel has inflicted on the earth a whimsical penitence in expiation of her intellectual fooleries. She has willed that during the whole duration of the reign of moral constraint upon the earth, her adaptations to this planet should be marked with the seal of her political antipathy. *Furens quid fœmina possit!* To this end she has ignobly travestied the cast of her aromas, and so well that the terrestrial emblems of Love now only figure as a laughable masquerade, and it has become excessively difficult to guess the hieroglyphics of Love even when we are forewarned of this. Not contented with the success of this perfidy, Herschel has pushed irony even to cruelty. She was the natural reservoir of blue flowers in her capacity of Cardinal Hyperminor. She has abused her position to refuse the perfume of Love to the flowers of this color, and has inoculated them in exchange with the perfume of pharmacy and *moral* properties, as the gentian.

"Thus the gamut of earth flowers is almost destitute of the blue note, and claims in vain by the eloquent pen of Alphonse Karr, the blue rose or the blue carnation—adjourned until the complete expurgation of the moralist virus. In place of the blue carnation, we may console ourselves with the borage, a charming flower of celestial blue, but which purifies the blood and makes no bouquets. The precious presents which Herschel has made the earth during the period of their cordial understanding, suggest the treasures we have lost by the rupture. Let us cite coffee, the truffle, the tuberose, the iris, the carnation, the hortensia, among plants; the sapphire among minerals; the swan, the turtle dove, ring dove, humming-bird, swallow, pheasant, partridge, thrush and quail, among birds.

"A delicate and sweet aroma, less intoxicating than those of Love, characterizes the creations of our unfortunate planet, whose concurrence is therefore so earnestly reclaimed by all the stars of the solar system. It is the aroma of the Violet—friendship; of the jessamine, reseda and vine. Most of those fragrant plants which interlace themselves over trees to form bowers, emanate from the aromas of the Earth. The title of fidelity and devotion characterizing the creations of this miniature cardinal, inspires a powerful interest in its unhappy lot. There is perhaps no star in heaven whose return to health and sanity is expected with more impatience, for the entire system suffers in its pangs, and the cardinal of Love, which now shows so much ill will towards the poor forsaken one, is perhaps she who will welcome her return to grace with greatest joy. Let us reflect that violet flowers, certain delicious perfumes, and choice wines, may be as rare in Herschel as fragrant blue flowers on our earth—that they are greatly desired in Herschel, and that the desires of a cardinal of Love must be still more intense than those of a cardinal of friendship!"—*Toussenel. Passional Zoology.*

THE VIOLET.

BY BARRY CORNWALL.

" I love all things the seasons bring,
All buds that start, all birds that sing,
All leaves, from white to jet;
All the sweet words that summer sends,
When she recalls her flowery friends,
But chief—the Violet!

" I love, how *much* I love the rose,
On whose soft lips the South-wind blows,
In pretty, amorous threat;
The lily, paler than the moon,
The odorous, wondrous world of June,
Yet more—the Violet!

" She comes, the first, the fairest thing
That Heaven upon the earth doth fling,
Ere Winter's star has set:
She dwells behind her leafy screen,
And gives, as Angels give, unseen,
So, love—the Violet!

" What modest thoughts the Violet teaches,
What gracious boons the Violet preaches,
Bright maiden, ne'er forget!
But learn, and love, and so depart,
And sing thou, with thy wiser heart,
'*Long live the Violet!*' "

ORANGE is the color of the *composite* character, whose passional tone blends different elements in enthusiastic concert as the orange blends and harmonizes the red and yellow shades. The tree, whose fruit gives name to this color, is the emblem of enthusiastic labor and generous profusion. It presents throughout the year an evergreen brilliant and rich scented foliage with bridal coronets of pure white flowers exhaling the most delicious aroma, and fruit in all the stages of growth and perfection at once. The soul overflows with a harmony before which our language throbs voiceless, in presence of this Passional Queen of the flower world. Sense and Spirit at once render their charmed allegiance to this symbol of absolute loveliness, power, pride, grace, and spontaneity. It is a living Pæan, a triumphal ode, springing concrete and organic, like all the thoughts of Suns and Planets, fresh from the heart of Earth in her bridal zone of the Tropic, in the plenitude of her Solar life. Its industrial analogies are expressed in the delicate finish and perfume of the leaf, indicating refinement and charm in the occupations of the character depicted, and in the nurture that has cherished its infancy and childhood. The practical results of the plant are expressed in its fruit and wood, its flower is all consecrated to beauty and to charm. It is in the flower only that the tree attains its own self-consciousness, the flower which is the fullness of its sensorial life in which it feels, loves, and enjoys—the flower which is its language ; which utters in odor, color and form, the glorious Word of this plant's revelation to Man. It tells me of our Passional Destiny, of our Paradise regained, of the real intentions of God, that man, as richly endowed by nature, should like this flower and its tree, be born and grow amid a sphere, a climate, an environment of harmonies responding to that divine ideal that he bears within him, and from whose chords every lovely thing in nature wakes music.

Its color is brilliant white, because the character it types blends every passional accord—Love, Ambition, Friendship, Kindred, the fascination of Sense and adoration of Soul—no tone is here deficient. Passion dawns in the blushing roses of the North, but its noonbeams glow in the orange of the tropics, and build an amaranthine throne in their evergreen bowers. (Enthusiasm is in place when we treat of the plant hieroglyphic of enthusiasm.)

Let us observe in the blossoming orange branch, the graceful pride of hierarchy in which its flower clusters rise above each other into a graduated cone or pyramid with well defined apex, like the flower of the Spanish bayonet (type of the castled baron of the feudal ages, living in inaccessible state and military honors), which presents this form in the highest degree, but without the manifold charms which mutually exalt each other in the composite orange, which is not however without its strong thorn of defence repelling familiarities. The cone is the most perfect of forms. The line that winds round from its base to its summit, describes the spiral of progression and persistent aspiration. You have the four conic sections, the Circle of Friendship, the Ellipse of Love, the Hyperbole of Ambition, and the Parabola of Familism, all presented in the different sections of which the cone admits. I admire the profusion of leaf, flower, and fruit, which this strong yet delicate branch sustains in their noble order without crowding them upon each other. We have here room for expansion, and a graceful flowing spontaneity without disorder, of which the dahlia and the camelia japonica, flowers of aristocratic pride and state, may well be envious, since in them liberty is sacrificed to order. So enchanting a combination of Harmonic effects was reserved for the hieroglyphic of attractive industry in the Passional Series, animated by enthusiasm in all its groups, who give to labor a soul, and to the sympathies of affection a body or incarnation, by arrangements which we have elsewhere explained in detail. The marvellous beauty and impassioned fragrance of this flower, fruit and tree, give us entirely the conception of that charm which will reign in the harmonious organizations of industry and society in the order of our destiny, where the Composite passion rules supreme, blending matter with spirit in the true incarnation. It may occur to some one that I here confound the orange tree with the color orange. The preceding connection of thought is perfectly just. The fruit resumes in itself the character of the tree, and the color of the fruit is physiognomical of that character.

GREEN is the color of unripe fruits, of the leaf elaborating juices which are to pass into the wood or other parts before they accomplish their ultimate purpose. It is the color of transition or of *work and change*, and corresponds with the Papillon or alternating passion, which reigns in the work of the Passional Series. The correspondence of green with mutation first struck me many years ago in observing the little green lizard which sports in our grape vines in Carolina.

How freshly I remember those summer days, some eighteen years ago, when I used to nestle in the cool bower of muscadine at the end of our long piazza, and the Grecian Mythology lessons, amid whose fantastic metamorphoses those pretty lizards used to divert me from my study whilst they served as living commentaries on it by their own fitful changes of color.

We were then three papillons together. The Greek Proteus, the chameleon, and the child sporting from object to object, and thus tending to a rich and true development which stupid driveling schools have since too well succeeded in stopping.

WHITE is the color of light, in which all colors blend, as all passions blend in the desire of Unity, in the sentiment of the spiritual Sun. It is also the color of *truth*, light being in the aromal sphere, and in its effects upon matter, what truth is in the spiritual sphere, and in its effects upon the soul. Light gives us the sensuous perception of physical objects, as truth intellectually of psychical objects anterior to their physical expression or embodiment. Light is essential to the development of organized structures. In proportion to its influence in the physical, as of science or truth in the psychical world, we have more perfect forms of organization, and better characterized expressions of each organic type. Contrast the comparatively rudimental structure of the mole, of the eyeless fishes in the underground streams of Kentucky, of the slimy reptiles disclosed by removing a rock or plank under which they have lived excluded from the light, with the higher organic types in which light has more fully cooperated.

Remark the feebleness or absence of their characteristic juices in etiolated plants. Watch in the laboratory how long substances possessing a strong affinity for each other will remain mingled but uncombined while light is excluded. These assert in the animal, in the vegetable, in the mineral sphere, the same principle which regulates human passions and human efforts towards ultimating them. The senses and affections act vainly, or produce only monstrosities, without the intervention of science or truth, of spiritual light, through the faculties of the intellect which are the eyes of the passions. Light being essential to the development of life, is at the same time the cause of chemical transformations and of the corresponding passional changes, since all the states of the soul have their basis in states of the body and its organic structures, and as in virtue of their special constitutions and capacities for the reception of light, bodies take every varied shade of color from indigo to white; so truth, in differently constituted and unequally developed minds, produces every varied shade of opinion. This we observe in the various and apparently contradictory religions which are all effects of one great truth, the instinct of Deity, expressing itself under these different forms or phases as one sect or one nation has appreciated some part of it, and one another, in awaiting the day which shall blend them in the church of Unity as the colors meet in White.

An intimate relation seems to exist between the pure colorless solar light, the white, or effect produced by the simple reflection of that light from an opaque medium, and the color blue, which is an atmospheric refraction of the same solar light. This relation is the natural cause of the harmony which white and blue, or translucent gauzes, lace, and other similar fabrics give with azure in dresses. I have observed the preference of these colors and combinations by impassioned women while modulating in the gamut of love.

In the heavens it is highly interesting to observe the Sun as a lover, and the manner in which our atmosphere reveals in the changing firmament of each zone and season the passional relation in which he stands with the Earth, giving every shade of azure mingled with pure white light and translucent cloud draperies, with now and then a storm by way of lover's quarrel. Indeed the Solar ray evinces the most profound respect for the passive or female principle, matter, since his rays give neither heat, color, nor chemical forces, until they meet and blend with the earth on its very surface.

These rays have traversed ninety-five millions of miles in space without creating anything, and it is permitted to us in making the moderate ascent of five miles upon mountain heights, where we come to air too thin for us to breathe, to reach a point where the bright blue of the firmament disappears in a dark void above us, and the green splendors of Earth's fairest gardens give place to the glacier and flee before the eternal ice breath, where all forms of living organisms cease, and the very elements fade into uncertain and ghost-like existence on the confines of vacuum.

Descending from these altitudes of eternal death and frost, it grows brighter and warmer as we near the extended surface of the earth ; the deep joyous smile of infinite tenderness ignoring and charming all our little sorrows, beams again round our planet cradle from the blue embracing firmament, and " Heaven bends low and breathes into our heart," as form after form of real empassioned life, foliage and flower, bird and chamois start into existence round us, and we listen to the still lingering tones of that spheral harmony which called all life from chaos in the gray morning twilight of Earth !

It is only when accompanying the Solar ray in its descent, we reach the plains and valleys again, that the teeming hosts of bird and beast, insect and creeping thing, with the exhaustless wealth of virgin soil, prairie forest, brake and swamp, issue from his intense embrace, and we are lost again in the positive infinite of real and concrete life, as before in the negative infinite of blank space and elementary dissolution.

Each spring as it renews the life of the earth commemorates that epoch when the stars sang together at the birth of their little sister. Germs and seeds that slept, now unfold into being, and the birds, our mother Earth's winged poesy, repeat the songs she teaches them in those hours of rapture, when she, like them, melts on the heart of her radiant lover.

EDGEWORTH.

"PERFUME—CHARM."

"Pleasure sits in the flower cup, and breathes itself out in fragrance."
RACHEL VARNHAGEN.

BY SARAH HELEN WHITMAN.

As the fabled stone into music woke
When the morning sun o'er the marble broke,
So wakes the heart from its stern repose,
As o'er brow and bosom the spring wind blows.
So it stirs and trembles as each low sigh
Of the breezy South comes murmuring by,
Murmuring by like a voice of love,
Wooing us forth amid flowers to rove,
Breathing of meadow paths thickly sown
With pearls from the blossoming fruit trees blown,
And of banks that slope to the southern sky,
Where languid violets love to lie.

No foliage darkens the wood path now,
No vine wreaths swinging from bough to bough,
But a trembling shadow of silvery green
Falls through the young leaf's tender screen,
Like the hue that borders the snowdrop's bell,
Or lines the lid of an Indian shell;
There the gold cup may burnish her crown all day,
As she basks in sunshine beside the way,
The anemone open her sleepy eye
To look at the clouds as they wander by,
Or lurk in the shade of a palmy fern
To gather fresh dews in her waxen urn.
Already the green budding birchen spray,
Winnows the balm from the breath of May,
And the aspen thrills to a low sweet tone,
Breathed for her listening ear alone.
In the tangled coppice the dwarf oak weaves
Its fringe-like blossoms and crimson leaves,

And the velvet buds of the willow unfold
Into downy feathers bedropt with gold ;
While thick as the stars in the midnight sky,
In the dark wet meadows the cowslips lie.

A love tint flushes the wind flower's cheek,
Rich melodies gush from the violet's beak,
In the drift of the rock the wild columbines grow—
Their heavy honey cups bending low,
As a heart which vague sweet thoughts oppress,
Droops 'neath its burden of happiness.

There the waters drip from their moss-fringed wells,
With a sound like the tinkling of silver bells,
Or fall with a mellow and flute-like flow
Through the channeled clefts of the rock below;
Soft music gushes in every tone,
And perfume in every breeze is blown ;
The flower in fragrance, the bird in song,
The glittering wave as it glides along,
All breathe the incense of boundless bliss,
The eloquent music of happiness.

And the soul as it sheds on this sun-bright hour
The untold wealth of its mystic dower,
Linked to all nature by chords of Love,
Lifted by faith to pure worlds above,
How with the passion of beauty fraught
Shall it utter its burden of blissful thought?

Yet sad would the spring-time of nature seem
To the soul that wanders mid life's dark dream,
Its glory a meteor that sweeps the sky,
A blossom that floats on the storm-wind by,
If as it passes on arrowy wing
It left not a token of endless spring;
If it nurtured no balm-breathing blossom of love,
To bloom for the amaranth garlands above.

THE LOVE-LADEN CARNATION.

The Carnation types a being who breathes only love, a class that love weighs down and enervates, since the carnation, its emblem, sinks and drags to the earth its elegant stalk; a friendly hand must come to sustain it, to marry it to a guardian twig.

Such is the young girl in the flush of glowing youth.

Oppressed by the burden of love, she yields like the carnation; her health even suffers, the necessity of passion surmounts in her the obstacles of education and position; and by analogy, the carnation, in a calyx crammed with petals, bursts its calyx surrounding, and escapes in disorder, letting fall its petals (symbols of pleasure). The hand of man must aid it in breaking the barrier of its calyx, and gently enclasping, favor the development of the petals.

So needs the empassioned girl for the full development of pleasure, the tender restraint of marriage, to save her love from suicide, by wantonness and waste. Thus aided, the flower is pompous, magnificent; and it is to paint to us faithfully this need of protecting husband and tender cares, that the carnation sinks under the weight of its flower, and asks of us the double aid of supporting stem and surrounding band. Details would run on to infinitude if we proceeded to the complete analysis of a vegetable picture,—to dissert upon the forms of the roots or seeds, on the habits and epochs of development, on parallels and contrasts. Why, for instance, between the rose and the carnation;

is the indenture fringed upon the leaves of the rose, and in contrast on the petals of the carnation? Why is the thorn placed on the stalks of the rose, whilst in the carnation it is the leaf which terminates in a point? These dispositions are emblems of the effects of love and of education amongst opulent maidens, for here it is not the poor class which is painted. When nature would depict the effects and characters of poverty, she must place them like the broom or the furze, in desolate spots; but when a flower or a fruit adorn the bodice of a belle or the table of a sybarite, their plants represent the peculiar passions and characters of the rich class. The Creator is a very faithful painter—he commits no errors. Comparative psychology is a science as vast as it is charming. It will fill at least a thousand large volumes for the vegetable kingdom alone, and the ladies will here contest the palms of renown, since each solution of these numberless enigmas may be coupled with the name of its fair decipherer. This beautiful science will banish the relish for *simple* exercises of ingenuity, like the riddles and charades of our newspapers and souvenirs. They will give place to enigmas which are composite, or allied with our passions and characters. Let us continue with flowers in favor, the roses and lilies.

THE LILIES AND THEIR LESSONS.

Nature, in her emblems, is almost indiscreet, from the very fidelity of her pencil, especially in the vegetables and animals symbolic of truth, as the lily, the pine tree, the swan, the stag, and the giraffe. Observe this indiscretion, first, in the lily flower. Its stalk is straight and firm, like the course of a truthful man. It is distinguished by a surrounding of graceful leaves —thus the honorable and truthful man shines by the marks of esteem which surround him in all his transactions, industrial or administrative, (leaf and work are synonymous.)

The corolla is like that of the tulip (emblem of the just man), a triangle without calyx. The conduct of the true and just veils itself in no mystery, and walks open to the day; thus the bulbous root of the lily everywhere opens in detached scales, and allows its interior to be seen, in analogy with the loyal man, whose principles and inmost sentiments show themselves, as through a window in his breast.

This flower, emblem of purity and rectitude, has two whimsical properties: it is treacherous, and it lives in banishment. First, it is perfidious, in bedaubing with a yellow powder whomsoever seduced by its perfume, approaches too near it. The soiling, which draws laughter upon its victim, represents the fate of those who familiarize themselves with truth.

Let a man, docile to the lessons of our moralists, and resolved to practice the august truth, which is, they tell us, the best friend of the human race, go into a saloon to tell the free and full truth about what the company present have done or are doing—the extortions of business men, and the secret intrigues of the ladies; he shall be treated as a philosophic barbarian, a churl, inadmissible to good company. Every one, by an invitation to the door, will prove to him that august truth is by no means the best friend of mortals, and can only conduct its too earnest devotee to disgrace. Nature writes us this lesson in the pollen with which she covers the stamens of the lily. It would seem that she would say to him whom this flower attracts—beware thou of truth ; do not rub thyself against it. This is the meaning of the smear that she draws over those imprudent noses which rub themselves carelessly against the lily flower, and get pointed at presently by the children, as we get ourselves pointed at by the fathers, when we dare to speak to them the august truth.

2d.—*The banishment of the lily.*—Truth is beautiful—yes, but beautiful to be seen at a distance ; and such is the opinion of the great world, since it cannot admit the flower of truth. We shall hardly present a bouquet of lilies to a lady of fashion ; we shall see no lily in the parlor of a Crœsus. All lovely as this flower is, its form, its perfume, its translucent white, befit not the class of Sybarites. They like the lily and truth only at a distance. They banish it to the corners of the flower-bed. In bouquet it only suits the people who have no fear of weighty truth. Thus may we see the lily displayed at public festivals, or at the door of humble inn, where truth presides. It charms children who fear not the full and frank truth. In Catholic countries it is used to adorn the statues and pictures of saints on the feast days ; and they do well to place the symbol of truth in the hands of the inhabitants of heaven, for if it is in fashion in the other world, it is by no means so in this. Other emblems of truth are varied in the species of this flower; the orange colored lily represents another class of the lovers of truth; those atrabilious misanthropes who practice it rudely, and know not how to make it amiable; so has this lily the characters of austerity. It has no perfume (charm). Its color is that of severe enthusiasm, the deep orange, —a dull shade—black spots.

TIGER-LILY.

The tiger-lily, in which these characters are most strongly marked, presents to us the portrait of the radical reformer.

It is accordingly, in New England, where such characters chiefly abound, that this flower seems to be a general favorite, and is commonly seen as an ornament or a scarecrow (according to our taste), in small village and country gardens. The whole aspect of this flower is most threatening and savage. Its petals coil back like a wild beast in act to spring. Its mottled spots and dark contrasts of color resemble those by which nature warns us to beware of danger in the leopard, and in many venomous snakes and poisonous plants.

Its pistil and stamens protrude far out of the flower-cup, denoting that delicacy is quite superfluous in the manners and proceedings of this class, and its very seeds stand out like black buckshot in the open axillæ of the leaves, as if ready to be discharged at you in their righteous indignation. It is truth, indeed, that the reformer speaks, and justice that he wishes, in the abolition of slavery, of intemperance, of land monopoly, or cannibalism; but he tells his truth in such a fashion as if he would be much disappointed at anything short of a good fisticuff of arguments and hard words; he deals much more with persons than with facts, and frequently is blinded by his combative enthusiasm, to the positive methods of accomplishing his end. Such has been the error of the Abolitionists, who, with the money and zeal they have expended in barking at the slaveholders, might have purchased plantations and negroes at the South, and there instituted experimental farms and manufactories, in which the superior profits of well-organized labor would not only have enabled them to emancipate, gradually, the negroes they had purchased, whilst developing them in character and practical resources, but by the system of ransoms divided into 6ths and 12ths, might have made of emancipation a good speculation, and actually enriched themselves, while determining through the love of personal interest, emancipation throughout the Southern States. There have been doubtless a few leaders, who have pocketed something as it is, which renders them the better satisfied to do nothing but bark. This is, however a very inverse sort of speculation, adding little to the power of the North or the freedom of the South.—Edgeworth.

THE WATER-LILY.

The loveliest of all the lilies is an emblem of that character which comes into truth through beauty. The family to which it belongs are in general emblems of truth in *action*, but this, rather of truth in *being*.

Root or Source.—The root of the water-lily, bedded in mud, has first an envelope of fine capillary down like the fur of a mole, which imbibes and secretes the elements of its growth; as from the moral filth of the lowest stations, the Being, like Sue's Fleur de Marie, is enabled to find spiritual food adapted to its life. They terminate in a cortex, like the outer layer of the brain or kidney. Irregular masses of spongy tissue next form cellular reservoirs, intersected by denser tissue. Only a careful dissection can expose these compartments, and the functions to which they minister; for in the character of this stamp, nature is at no pains to expose to the vulgar eye the sources of her working. We see only the result, the perfect flower of being, sitting queen-like upon the waters of life; and wrapt in the miracle of its presence, we forget to ask whence it sprung, or what were the steps of its attainment.

The Leaves—organs of work—spring directly from the root, disconnected from the flower stem, though through the intervention of the vascular tissue at its source, they contribute to it the elements elaborated from the air, and at the surface of the water.

"Consider the lilies how they grow; they neither

toil nor spin, yet Solomon in all his glory was not arrayed like these."

The Being here depicted, is one not formed for the coarser uses of life. It has a higher use,—to embody the results of labor.

The Doer is in the leaf, the Being in the flower of life's growth.

In states of motion, action, struggle; destiny is not yet proportioned to attraction; the actual has not yet reached the ideal: thus the leaf, the organ in which the plant chiefly performs its labors of elaboration for the uses of the flower and fruits, is green. the color of alternation or transition.

The proportion of destiny to attraction, the embodiment of the ideal in the actual, is comparatively a state of rest, rather than motion; of being, rather than action; of beauty, rather than force. Characters of this class fulfill the highest purposes in apparent idleness; from the pivot of their own life, they exert attractions, instead of following the attractions of others, and they influence with a quiet charm, like the aroma of the flower, waking into life a sentiment and impulse towards the beautiful and the true that slumbered beneath the worldly crust of other characters.

In society, considered as a whole, there are classes of characters adapted like the different members or organs of a single plant or animal, to specific positions or functions; so that in the order for which God has calculated them, each brings to the great serial life, individual qualities which no other possesses, and without ever a collision of interest from dissimilitude of character; variety in the parts being the essential condition of unity in the whole. Each molecule obeying its own attractions, and each tissue or organ in filling the special function based upon those attractions, enables other molecules and groups of molecules in the tissues, or groups of tissues in the organs, to obey their several attractions, and fill their functions in the serial order, in full security that general well-being will arise from this wise selfishness. Some, corresponding to the muscle or the leaf, must be chiefly hewers of wood and drawers of water; others, like authors and artists, perform the function of glands which secrete from the common torrent of life-blood, products of specific character; a third class correspond to the sensory nervous system; these are the beings now before us, who, without moving, are the cause of motion in others. The sensory nervous center to which they correspond, is indirectly connected with the working organs through commissures of nerve fiber, as the flower in which the lily presents her developed life, connects indirectly with the leaf elaborating its elements, through a vascular network in the root. This want of immediate connection indicates that the character represented needs no immediate assistance from the drudgery of education, as it is conducted amongst us, but blooms self-developed. It is only at its source in the root that it receives the products elaborated, as the knowledge gained through the parent's intellect and fixed in the habit of his thought or life, is organized in the structure of his child with the sensibility of a spiritual instinct. The education or cares preparing the development both of the lily and the being, act thus through organization, rather than by direct communication. The leaf in itself conforms to the general type of this character—floating in large circles gracefully upon the waters, concealing its red spongy gill tissue below the surface, and glistening above with polished verdure.

The *Stalk* or *Course*—is not stiffly upright like that of the other lilies,—of the pine tree, &c., emblems of simple truth. The being which it types avoids struggle and oppositions as the lily yields to the current, whilst preserving internally its directness of aim as the lily its linear stem free from knots ; bending sometimes, but never crooked, and in its very curve conforming to the line of beauty.

Calyx and *Corollà.*—The garden lily has none, by analogy with the openness of a simply truthful character which wears round its pleasures as the plant round the flower of its life,—no clothes or concealments. The water-lily, in conformity with the shrinking delicacy of its human analogue, protects from the drifting slime, with a graceful calyx of its own petals thickened, the temple of its love and of its treasures ; as the sensitive *being* conceals what is most sacred in her life from lower creatures that might defile and could not comprehend it, but opens herself above to the eye of Heaven, or to that of man, when with worthy devotion he comes to seek her in her own sphere. Her truth is not uttered to all ears, nor in public places, nor is her voice earnest in season and out of season. Thus it is only in the morning freshness, when nature breathes, and sings, and flutters her orison to God, that this flower opens the dome of her corolla. It is pure translucent white, the sacred color of unity, in which all other colors blend, as all passions converge in the aspiration toward God. It has not the triangular form of another lily, which types the great truth of nature—Tri-unity.

The Water-Lily conforms here again to the type of the beautiful,—preeminently expressed in the circles of its flower—a form the most lovely to us by natural adaptation, and from its consonances, with that of our mother's breast, which teaches the infant eye its first lesson of beauty; with that of the green hills upheaving their swelling bosoms in the landscape that next greets us with God's good-morning; with the sphere of the dew-drop and the star; with the disk of the Sun; and above all, with the human eye,—where contrasted with the ellipse of the brow and lids, with the triangle of the nose, brow, and cheek-bone, with the line of the mouth, the hyperbola of the forehead above, and the parabola of the chin below, lies bedded in pearl, the round iris, from whose radiant orbit the soul looks out.

NOTE.—Every creature is, 1st—a material body; 2d—a series of vital attractions; 3d—an order in which those vital forces move, so as to form regularly its internal functions, and to constitute its specific type of being. God is analogically a Trinity, embracing 1st, the passive principle—matter; 2d, the active principle—will, passion or universal attraction; 3d, the neuter principle—order, or the mathematics of creation.

The same graceful roundness and freedom from those angular traits of character which bring us into collision with others, marks the manners of the self-poised, self-concentred being, who acts by silent influences, by showing quietly the true and beautiful in her own life. In accordance with this inobtrusiveness, repeated in every feature of the being and of the flower, this lily does not, like others of its family, smear with the pollen of projecting stamens, the imprudent noses which approach it. We may draw nearer to truth expressed in beauty, without incurring the penalty of ridicule, or fearing to be pointed at.

The beings here depicted always present truth, so that it is loved and taken home. Thus this lily offers a highly prized, though not a common nor an easily gathered bouquet.

The perfume of this species is very rich and composite. Its aroma does not, like the rose or yellow jessamine, excite the intoxicating charm of human passion. It is like the first aspiration that morning bears with its own perfume from the fountain of sweet thoughts, welling up from a pure, fresh, quiet heart.

The *stamens*—organs of production—in conformity with the truthfulness of the character, are of a clear yellow, manifesting the true color of paternity, the same with that of the seed or ripened grain, the fruit or product to be obtained. There is an innocent deception practiced by this flower, typing the exquisite refinement of the being, about what she holds in herself most sacred. It is the concealment of the stamens and pistil beneath a double row of small petals, simulating in shape and color the stamens round which they form a lovely canopy. The Japanese mythology, enraptured by this chaste arrangement, placed the throne of love within the dome of a Nymphæa.

This plant retires to lone and quiet spots, to open its flowers on the still waters, far from the interference of the gardener, as the Being is most genially developed away from conventional teachings, among the sweet, wild influences of nature, where—

> " She may lean her ear in many a secret place,
> Where rivulets run their wayward round,
> And beauty born of murmuring sound,
> May pass into her face."

Inhabiting the element of truth—water ; possessing the color of unity—white ; the typical form of beauty—round—repeated in its stem, leaf and corolla, externally, and internally in the tubes of its stalk and the dome of its corolla : with its peculiar ineffable aroma, and its entire chasteness, the water-lily has eminently characters which must entitle it to a place among the sacred emblems used in divine worship ; when religion casting off as a slough, the austere mask, the sackcloth, and the horrid rods of vengeance which she has borne through purgatorial ages, shall ally herself with the beautiful, and see in God our friend and the Author of attraction, and in man the grateful child, fulfilling his destiny by obeying his attractions in the divine social order.—EDGEWORTH.

The tulip and the lily are contrasted hieroglyphics of honor; the tulip in its simple, and the lily in its compound development;—*i. e.*, the former exclusive of power and interest, the latter connected with them.

Now what do we mean by honor? Among civilized people it consists in successful frauds, speculations, stock-jobbing, &c. Among barbarians, in pillaging, oppressing, destroying. Among savages, in killing the bravest of other tribes, wearing their scalp locks as trophies, or drinking warm blood from their skulls.

According to the instincts of nature, it consists in the practice of justice, truth, and productive industry.

The tulip, which portrays simple honor, has generally instead of perfume, a bitter odor. It is the emblem of man's actual fate:—he who practices justice and truth reaps only bitter disappointments, and is, though an admirable character at a certain distance, repulsive by his frankness. Thus the world fears the approach of a just, free, and severe man; the tulip which depicts him, ought by analogy, to have a repulsive aroma which obliges us to admire it at a distance, like the lily, dangerous by its pollen.

We have seen that the pollen of the lily is a snare which exposes the unwary to ridicule. It soils the face of those who smell at the flower, exposes them to be pointed at, and laughed at, as happens to every one who grows too familiar with truth, is blindly impassioned for it, and determines on speaking it openly in a hypocritical world, where it is not admissible; and in order to depict faithfully the ridiculous side of this enthusiasm for truth, the lily smears with orange, the color of enthusiasm, those who eagerly smell the perfume of truth in the lily.

The pollen or seminal dust of the tulip is not orange but brown, the color of defeat or of mourning, that of the dead leaf.

To rear one's children to the practice of strict justice is generally a legacy of defeat in the practical business of civilization—thus the tulip wears this allegorical character. Some will reply and sustain that a wise father can, without compromising the interest of his children, rear them to justice,—but to what sort of justice? to cupidity, oppression and falsehood, smoothed over by the name of prudence; as to true justice, every child reared to practice it without reserve, will soon arrive at his ruin.

The aroma of compound honor, furnished by the lily, is a very strong odor, which few can bear.

Whence is it that the perfume of compound honor is not abortive in the lily as that of simple honor in the tulip? It is because honor becomes very practicable, and even very brilliant when combined with authority and grandeur, portrayed by the lily, which is king among flowers, as the lion among quadrupeds. A minister devoted to honor, a Sully, a truly just and loyal man, shines even in a false world with great luster. But Sully, shorn of his power, and brought back into private life, will find in the practice of truth and justice, only pledges of proscription. Sully will have passed from the part of the lily into that of the tulip ; he will always shine by his virtues, but not attract,—rather repel by his moral severity ; thus the tulip is imposing by its colors, but repulsive by the bitter perfume of its cup.

It has often been said that the just is obliged to turn away his eyes and wrap himself in his cloak. This withholding of sympathy is represented by the privation of perfume.

We censure the tulip for its bitter odor ; this is to accuse our society, because it does not admit the free expression of honor, or the practice of justice and truth in the private individual. The star which gives us this flower, has then acted as a faithful painter in the tulip as in the lily, in refusing to one the fragrance it has granted to the other, to that which is allied with authority and power. [We have now, at least in the United States, highly fragrant tulips. I have seen several varieties in the garden of Mr. Simpson, of Providence, R. I. This fact is analogy with the progress of liberty, which in our republican societies permits a free expression of honor and truthfulness in the private individual.]—E.

Let us follow these two flowers in other characters, where we shall see justice peculiarly typed in the tulip, and truth in the lily. Truth *in the rich and powerful* has a noble and majestic tone ; thus the stalk of the lily is firm, straight, and noble, like the course of a truthful man, when he has *power and fortune*, which are depicted by the luxury of leaves with which the stalk is provided, and by its great firmness. The stalk of the tulip is equally seductive in its polish and its graceful shading, but very brittle,—reminding us of the slight support which justice finds when practiced by an uninfluential person.

The bulbs are contrasted: that of the lily open, and showing all its work, emblematic of the truthful man, whose principles have nothing concealed; the other bulb, that of the tulip, is very compact and concentrated, as if it had been pressed in a mould: it is the emblem of justice, compressed by unfavorable circumstances in the social soil from which it springs.

We remark in both flowers the same character of loyalty, in the absence of the calyx or envelope. Nothing hidden in the course of just and true men; no mask, no distrust; thus act the tulip and the lily,—they give us their splendid flowers without the precaution of the mysterious preserving envelope, or calyx.

The truly loyal and just man disdains those measures which prudence might suggest to others. Strong in his own conscience, he proceeds with head erect in all his operations. Thus the lily and the tulip go frankly to their ends without enveloping in any mystery their principal operation, which is no other than flowering, since their only end is to give a majestic flower.

The forms of the flower are those of justice, the triangular; emblem of Divine justice in its three attributes (Universal Providence, Distributive Justice, and Expediency or Economy of Means). Their triangle is vertical in the tulip, horizontal in the largest variety of the lily.

The tulip is triangular in the assemblage of its three superior petals: when the unfolding of the three others allows them to be seen, it passes from the triangle to the circle, which is the second emblem of justice; thus the image of God is formed of these two figures—a triangle inscribed within a radiating circle.

The lily forms the triangle horizontally, by turning over the superior portion of the six petals. Thus the two flowers give still the same lesson in their contrasted expressions.

We shall again find this identity in the colors of the tulip and the lily. They must paint in contrast the two elements of honor—justice and truth.

Let us first seek the emblem of justice in the colors of the tulip; it excludes the two blues; azure, the color of the passion supremely unjust, which is love,—indigo, the color of the cabalistic or party spirit, enemy of justice in the present society. These two passions may, in the future, accord well with justice, hence the tulips of the next creation will not exclude the two blues, but they must be eliminated from the present tulip, which only represents ages of disorder. It does not admit the orange, symbol of blind enthusiasm (the exalting passion), which is incompatible with justice; it admits the yellow, although the family sentiment is amongst us one of the chief springs of injustice, but not so with the just man, who will not despoil the younger in favor of the elder, nor abandon his natural children. It suffices then that the tulip should exclude the two colors of the passions incompatible with justice, and that it should display with splendor the colors of the other passions which the just man uses so nobly.

The allegory of colors being sufficiently expressed in the tulip, there is no need that it should be repeated in the lily, which is limited to the color of Unity, white, and then to the orange color, whence it draws two portraits in the spotted lily and the weeping reversed lily. Of these three flowers, the white lily is the only one which possesses any charm.

Unity pleases wherever it reigns, whether in the sphere of the senses, where every one loves the unitary accord of orchestras, of military evolutions, &c., or in our spiritual pleasures, as the drama, where we require the concurrence of the three unities; and as truth is the principal lever of unity, all the charm must be given to that lily of the three, which depicts truth united with justice.

INODOROUS FLOWERS.

We now select the three inodorous flowers—The Lady Slipper, or Touch-Me-Not—hieroglyphic of the Industrious Egotist; Crown Imperial—the Unfortunate Artist, or votary of science; Hortensia—Extravagant Coquette. Every one knows the Lady Slipper, the reserve of the flower garden in late summer and fall. When we would gather its seed, collecting in our hand a dozen capsules, we no sooner close it than they fly open, surprise us into relaxing our grasp, and let the seed escape on all sides. The treasure is lost by the very eagerness with which we seek to retain it. Is not this a raillery of nature? To give us a product, and then take it away from us at the moment that we grasp it carefully. Explain the secret of this whim.

The Lady Slipper is the portrait of the industrious egotist. Egotism is a prevalent character amongst the rich who addict themselves to industry. The leaves, so finely indented and symmetrically distributed, are an emblem of intelligent labor. A tuft of leaves surmounts the flowers as a symbol of prudent and judicious economy, which will have the work, figured by the leaves, and the profit, to exceed the expense. Observing this method, it can shine very long without impoverishing itself, like the Lady Slipper, which yields a long series of flowers, abundant and splendid.

The household imbued with this refined prudence, is supremely ambitious and egotistical. Thus the Lady Slipper, its analogue, refuses all tribute to man. Its flowers can neither be gathered singly, from want of stem, nor in bunches, from the profusion of leaves. We gather them not for our boquets nor parlor vases; 'tis a plant that lives only for itself, like the households of rich egotists, giving style and tone to the country—active and influential persons, useful to the mass, but ungenial from their captious spirit—they render themselves necessary, like the Lady Slipper, without being either loved or lovable.

They know how to install themselves into all the avenues of greatness, like this flower, which gains possession of the most frequented spots of the garden, and there displays its splendor without charming. It is deprived of fragrance, the symbol of charm. It is late, a luxury of autumn, in allusion to those hoarders who do not begin till late to shine in the world. Spite of all their vigilance, their fortune chances to pass to improvident heirs, who squander it; thus the grain or inheritance of the plant escapes the hand at the moment we carelessly gather it. The flower will be more interesting in a parallel with its autumnal ally—

THE REINE MARGARITE—INDUSTRIOUS HOUSEWIFE.

The Reine Margarite is not a flower of the spring. It is not in the spring, but in the autumn of life that a woman becomes a skilful manager; so the emblematic flower of this character must be in our gardens the ornament of autumn. The true ornament of a housewife is the perfection which reigns in her numerous labors. She does not shine by dress, but by industry (leafwork). Thus has the Margarite for its principal ornament a mass of leaflets in its calyx. They differ from the leaves of the stalk, they are true petals of green color, and long develop themselves with infinite grace. We see that she would excite by her leaves that charm which others excite by their petals: then comes the flower more beautiful simple, than composite. A double Margarite is an absurdity, the single is preferable, like the tulip. It only supervenes to add another row, a crown to the green petals, whose graceful development has long charmed the eye. Thus among housewives a simple and modest dress is a sufficient accessory to the charm which the excellence of their work has caused. But this neatness of the housewife is only a charm for the mind and not for the heart; it is not a resource of pleasure. Hence, nature has refused this flower perfume, symbol of illusion and fascination.

We will examine that bed opposite the Lady Slipper. The active fortunate (intriguer) has been depicted. See now the portrait of noble industry humiliated. It is that of the votary of science or art. It is painted in the flower called

THE CROWN IMPERIAL,

Bearing six corollas reversed, and surmounted like the Lady Slipper, by a tuft of leaves. This flower, which has the form of truth, the triangular form of the lily and tulip; excites a lively interest by the accessory of six tears, which are found in the bottom of the calyx. Every one is surprised by it. It seems as if the flower was in sorrow, it hangs its head and sheds large tears, which it hides under its stamens. It is then the emblem of a class which suffers in secret. This class is very industrious, for the flower bears like a banner the sign of industry; the tuft of leaves grouped around the top of the stalk, symbolic of the high and noble industry of art and science. The class of laborers who sorrow in secret, is not that of the gross plebeians, but that of the useful men of science, forced to yield precedence to fortunate vice—thus doth the plant incline her lovely flowers in the posture of humility. They are swelled with hidden tears, an image of the lot of those workers in silence, who for the achievement of all that society holds most precious and beautiful, are paid by slights, whilst leeches and stockjobbers suddenly amass fortunes. This flower has the orange color of enthusiasm, in analogy with the industrious class of artists and men of science, who have no other support than enthusiasm against the poverty and the humiliations whose cup their youth must drain.

After the painful struggle in their early life, they attain some relief; some little enjoyment of their being. In imitation, the flower after passing its fresh beauty in an humble attitude, at last raises its peduncle and its capsule of grain; but it is too late to change when the peduncle, no longer adorned by its beautiful flower, has but a poor husk to display. This effect depicts the long deferred comfort of the artist and man of science who cannot raise their heads nor issue from the estate of constraint and oppression, until they have painfully consumed their youth in amassing a little money; after having bent in their youth under the weight of calumny, poverty, and injustice, and lost the glorious morning of life, in preserving its evening from indigence.

THE HORTENSIA,

Hieroglyphic of the fashionable coquette—displays a profusion of dress, more flowers than leaves. I have counted one hundred and eight balls on a Hortensia of moderate size. It is a plant which fatigues the eye by its masses of flowers, which it produces in the same excess as the coquette who would consume in finery the whole means of the household. By analogy, the Hortensia hides its leaves under a pile of inodorous and half shaded flowers, roseate or half rose, argentine or half blue, lilac or half violet; tints ambiguous, like the sentiments of the coquette, which are—

> A weak love, argentine not azure;
> A lukewarm friendship, lilac and not violet;
> A false modesty, roseate and not rose.

The Hortensia and the Lady Slipper (coquette and egotist), are two flowers which only live for themselves, and refuse contributions to the hand of the gatherer. We cannot employ cuttings of the Hortensia in bouquets on account of its bulk, or in vases, where it rapidly withers. Uncut and in flowerpots, it figures brilliantly in saloons and gardens, like the coquette in the fashionable world. It has no perfume, because the coquette dazzles the eye and fascinates the mind, without touching the heart. She charms the senses. The tie with man is simple, the charm of the flower must be simple,—pleasing the eye without attracting by its fragrance. The coquette ruins herself by luxury; and the Hortensia, by analogy, fears the Star of luxury and dies of a sun-stroke.

The coquette, in the decline of age, impoverished by foolish extravagance, is forced to resort to industry; in imitation, the Hortensia, after making a brillant display, loses its color, its luxury, and takes the shade of work—green, the color of the leaf. It only attains a faint green, because the coquette only gets up a sort of half industry, connected with intrigue. Finally, at an advanced age, she plays the part of a prude, and the Hortensia, by analogy, endues at the close of the season, the color of prudery—brown, the shade of the Scabious, which is the flower of prudery, rebellious to the hand that would gather it. Fashionable coquettes are women who have received a careful education, and as an emblem of this preparatory labor, Nature gives the Hortensia a leaf elegantly indented in symmetrical lozenges. The flower seems to be deprived of stamens and pistils ; 'tis the picture of the coquette who eschews the cares of matrimony. Thus the organs of reproduction are hidden in the Hortensia. This plant, to arrive at perfection, requires great attention ; its agricultural toilet is one of the most complex, like that of the personages represented.

An essential discrimination in this study is that of the eight Societies. (See the table, Note A.)

A plant representing some effect of barbarism is incomprehensible unless we understand the customs of barbarians ; and thus of the plants which represent the social effects of the sixth, seventh, and eighth periods, they will be incomprehensible to those who know nothing above civilization in the fifth period.

Flowers quite familiar to us, the jessamine, violet, heartsease, reseda, are pictures of the eighth period.

How can we treat of these analogies with a reader who knows not the customs of the eighth Society? To make them feel the necessity of studying the eighth period before studying its botanical analogies, I explain only one of the four flowers cited above. I choose the Reseda, much prized for its delicious perfume.

It represents the industrious children of the Societary order. (See Universal Unity, Vol. iv. Sections 3 and 4.*) Its flower has no visible petals, it is only composed of the productive part, stamens and pistil; in allusion to the children of harmony, unceasingly occupied with productive functions, and finding pleasure only in useful work, which they exercise in numerous passional series. By analogy, the Reseda suppresses the petals, emblems of unproductive pleasure. A very sweet perfume escapes from this floweret in symbol of the charm which children possess when passionately given to useful industry. Nature gives to the stamens the capucine shade, mixture of red and orange (colors of enthusiasm and of ambition), symbolical of the industrial lever of the harmonian children, which is an enthusiasm sustained by ambition.

Below the flowers, comes a long file of little sacs but partly filled and open. It is the emblem of all the little treasures which the harmonian child amasses, his expenses being small while he generally accumulates numerous savings from the dividends obtained in the different series which he has frequented. Their collection composes a little fortune which is placed at his.

* Park Godwin is now preparing this for the American press.

disposal about his fifteenth year of age. There is little grain in the capsules, because the child should gain only inconsiderable dividends in his series. Nature has left the sacs open, though turned mouth down; this is a double omission in prudential precautions by analogy with the impossibility of deceiving and despoiling a harmonian child, although he disdains every precaution against cunning and theft.

This picture can have no application to the manners of civilized children. We understand by it that it would be impossible to study vegetable and animal allegories as long as we are ignorant of the mechanism of the sixth, seventh, and eighth social periods, to which a great number of plants relate, such as the jessamine, violet, heartsease, reseda, serpentine, cacao; whose analogy does not exist in the customs and manners of civilization.

JONQUIL AND NARCISSUS.

In general, and with rare exceptions, half-inclined flowers are emblematic of the family or paternal and maternal ties, descending from the superior or stronger to the inferior or weaker being. They present the curve of the Parabola.

Amongst mothers, this affection is violent and blind; thus nature has endowed with an intense perfume the Jonquil, emblem of maternal love. This love is a charm which springs among troubles and cares; thus the flower rises through needle-shaped leaves.

It bears exclusively the colors of paternity—yellow;

its culture is excessively troublesome, in analogy with the cares of children. The plant is small, because it represents only the branch of affection and cares adapted to childhood.

The Narcissus, in its varieties, would depict to us different effects of the family bond, sometimes insipid, like the pale yellow, inodorous Narcissus; at others, very pleasant, as in the fragrant Narcissus.

THE CHERRY,

Image of the tastes of infancy, is one of the first fruits of the fine season. It is in the order of the fruit harvest what childhood is in the order of ages. The four species of fruit which the season yields us, follow the progression of the four phases of humanity. Friendship prevails in the first place, among children; and love in the second place, among adults. By analogy, the fruits typical of friendship should appear the first, and those of love next in the season. The strawberry and cherry are fruits of friendship and of childhood. The plum, apricot and peach, of love and adolescence.—To these succeed the pears, symbolic of ambition, which prevails in the third phase of virility,* and the progression is closed by the apple,

* It is remarkable in connection with this, that Bonaparte, perhaps the purest impersonation of ambition the world has seen, always instinctively chose this fruit as a metaphor; when speaking of his plans he was wont to say, "The *pear* is not yet ripe," or "the *pear* is now ripe."—E.

the emblem of the family sentiment, which prevails during the fourth phase, or old age.

The Cherry, portrait of free, happy, and sportive children, ought to excite in them the effects which it represents. Thus the appearance of a basket of cherries throws into transports the whole infantile tribe, to whom this fruit is very healthy. The cherry is a plaything which nature gives the child. He makes garlands and ear pendants of them, he crowns himself with them like Silenus with the vine. The tree is analogous to the genius and to the labors of infancy. It is sparsely furnished with leaves (at least in its natural state). Its branches, wide apart, give little shade, and neither ward off the rain nor the sun, image of the feeble means of infancy; it is incomplete, insufficient to protect and to shelter man.

The STRAWBERRY is the most precious of the early fruits. It depicts the child reared in harmony and in groups of industry. A strawberry plant is a worker who labors like our gardeners. Its running shoots plant in a straight line a row of suckers. It is just, that the most valuable of children, he who labors in conbined industry, should have for his emblem the most delicate fruit of the series.

The Strawberry will, like the Peach, combine agreeably with wine and with sugar, emblems of friendship and unity; thus labor in combined groups is sustained by friendship and tends to unity.

GOOSEBERRIES AND CURRANTS.

These berries represent different classes of children. The most notable is the red cluster Currant—the emblem of unrefined children, given up to their free nature. Their frankness is pungent and indiscreet—they are capable of running to repeat to a lady of pretension some mortifying truth which they have just heard of her. The fruit which types these little truth-tellers ought to have a very piquant flavor. It is pleasant because truth is graceful in a child, and amuses in spite of the indiscretion. Such a part is not without usefulness; it holds up faults to the light, and chastises by a laugh. Thus is the fruit of the red Currant purifying and wholesome. The plant resembles in its leaves and clusters the vine—emblem of composite friendship—thus are these free, prattling, indiscreet children those most addicted to simple friendship. This sort of Currant is a fruit of popular character, and is prized but moderately, like the class of children which it represents. It is seldom seen raw at good tables, we only make use of it by combining it with sugar and the cares of the conservatory; thus children too free and unpolished, come into favor only as they imbibe the manners of the more elevated and refined classes.

The thorny Gooseberry with single berries, depicts the child of constraint, deprived of pleasures, tormented with moral precepts, and reared in solitary study. Its emblem gives but a poor sort of fruit, pale violet, the color of abortive friendship, the development of which is obstructed in his nurture by isolating him from his companions. These children, puffed up with precepts and premature studies, generally grow up to be but indifferent characters. Thus the hieroglyphic fruit is, notwithstanding its fine looks, a product of small value, swelled with insipid juices and superfluous grains, like children who are surfeited with ill-digested learning. This gooseberry is thorny, as an emblem of the cramped and fretful temper of the unhappy children it depicts.

The Black Currant and Gooseberry represent poor and coarse children, thus the fruit is black—emblematic of privation, and of bitter and disagreeable taste, in analogy to the children of the rabble, who have the defects of bad language, bad manners, and often bad principles. They only become tolerable when refined by contact with the rich and polished class, and this berry likewise becomes eatable only by mixing with it brandy and sugar.

THE GRAPE VINE.

The Grape is of all plants that grow, the friendliest. Wine, in moderation, is truly the friend of man, it assists digestion, enlivens our guests, opens the heart, and is as healthful for the man as the fruit is for the child. The ripe grape of the finer varieties, and not eaten to excess, is a preservative from disease, and often a remedial agent. The vine, by a friendly analogy, will embrace our trees and our houses. It needs to associate, to form ties with all that stands near it, thus is it gifted with the tendril which is an attribute of friendship and alliance. It gives good fruit only when it is closely trimmed. This is an analogy with the groups of friendship in Society, which perfect themselves in industry by the continued exercise of a playful raillery, whose critical pruning-knife lops off and clears away faults whilst sustaining emulation.

The Grape is a late fruit, as is composite or collective friendship, which can only exist in that mature social state of which a globe is only susceptible after long travail in periods of limbo, ages of perplexed social beginnings and of painful industry ; the vine gives us the image of it in the tears—(bleeding), which precede its growth of leaves. The fruit represents a series or combination of groups, an arrangement whence friendship springs. It is formed of a series of little groups of distinct grapes. Its color is the violet, emblem of friendship ; and the white, emblem of unity.

In our democratic republic, Friendship may take a freer and more liberal development than in old and thick settled court-ridden countries. In our south and southwest especially, it festoons rich and exuberant as the grape vines of our forest over the open frame of our social institutions, connecting individuals and families in the most genial relations amid the spontaneous expansion of individual characters.

Our native vines, by analogy, scorn the critical pruning knife, and in their untrammeled energies spread over whole roods, from whose arbors the magnificent Scuppernong may be raked by the bushel, and whose vintages, surpassing the most sanguine dreams of the vigneron, have yielded at the rate of six thousand dollars' worth to the acre ! ! ! Hurra for Uncle Sam ! ! ! !

EDGEWORTH.

The vine loves to gossip. It is a fault which is common to it with the setter dog, and with many amiable persons of both sexes ; and in conscience it would be difficult to impute this charming weakness as a crime to a plant whose juice unties the tongue, and which is a cardinal emblem of friendship. In the ardor of expansion which consumes it, the vine attaches itself with love to all that surrounds it ; it climbs familiarly on the shoulder of plum trees, of olives, of elms—it enclasps all the trees. Since the vine modulates in the tone of friendship, its familiarity is legitimate. I had one for the friend of my childhood, a generous and prodigal friend whom I still see here stretch out to me its long arms loaded with fruits, fruits golden and purple, which waited to ripen in those happy days of September, when the young exile returns to his natal hearth, when the schoolmaster is mute that the red-throat may sing.

Its rich foliage, delight of the children, pride of the family, not content to garland with its net-work the southern face of an immense wall, had scaled its crest to be on neighborly terms by means of its most adventurous twigs with an espalier of the next house.

The most cordial understanding reigned between the

two trellises, and several circumstances which a gardener will guess without mentioning them, had contributed to draw its ties closer. But death one day entered the next house, then came a new master, who pretended to the right of adding a few feet to the height of the dividing wall, and who abused it.

It was then necessary to sever the tendrils which linked together the friendly espaliers. Their hearts long bled, and the barbarity soon showed its results. From the first autumn the harvest of both trellises diminished by half in weight and in flavor. The year after, the two stalks put forth only in wood, and increased in height with incredible energy. It was pitiful to see the stumps of hardened tendrils under the leaf, discolor the place where the bunches of translucid gold formerly displayed themselves in all the lustre of their appetizing beauty. Two or three years passed without bringing about any notable change in the disposition of the rebel espaliers.

Horticultural science vainly appealed to all the resources of vegetable therapeutics to conquer this obstinate barrenness.

Warm manures, foot baths, winter mantles of straw, caresses, minute attentions, nothing answers the purpose, or rather all is turned into wood. On both sides of the wall the disappointment reaches its acme, especially among the children. Idleness alone is sweet after ten months of unwilling labor in the garden of Greek roots; but indolence beloved of the Chasselas grape is far sweeter still. The old folks already speak of extreme measures, and pronounce the fiat of tearing up the vines, when one fine morning in April, the down of the buds of both trellises opens and allows a double gemmula to be seen issuing from its silky covering, unhoped-for promise of a rich harvest.

And as one of the proprietors was boasting of the success of his efforts, which had triumphed, if you might believe him, over the resistance of nature: "Father," asked his son, a child of twelve, who shared largely in his father's joy, "have you observed how the branches which they separated three years ago, have met above the wall, say?" The learned father took no account of the child's observation. Five months afterward, amid the joys of the harvest, the proprietor of the neighboring trellise repeated for the twentieth time to him, "Do you know that this is very queer, the coalition of these two vines, which give each other the word to *strike*, and then to resume bearing at the same time?"

"It is certainly very singular and inexplicable," replied my father, who was a learned man.

There have many dramas been made with convent walls, cloistered victims and silken ladders, not more interesting than these simple facts. The annals of passional botany which few have hitherto explored, swarm with similar histories and—remarkable circumstance;—The moral of these romances always says: God has placed us in this world to love and to enjoy; let us love, let us be happy, in order to please God.

Why did these two vines refuse to bear during three years? Because the attraction of the vine is to bind itself in friendship with all that surrounds it, to gossip about various matters. In separating the two friendly espaliers, in subjecting them to the order of the cloister, in condemning them to silence, a destiny had been forced on them, not proportional to their attractions. They rebelled, and refused to bear. They were in their right, and they re-entered the path of harmony and fecundity on the day when they re-entered the path of their attractions. These are, however, beings to which civilized science denies feeling.—TOUSSENEL.

The analogy of the grape vine naturally leads us to cross the threshold of Passional Hygiene, from my work on which I shall here borrow a few pages. In the combined order where culinary provisions are made for fifteen hundred or two thousand persons at once, a great number and variety of dishes will be prepared at every meal, the children as well as the adults forming table groups, each of which makes its own selections from the bill of fare; it will be convenient for children to have instincts, and as God seems to have been of the same opinion, since he never fails to distribute them, children will from a very early age be encouraged to choose, to express their preference, and to observe the adaptations of various diets to their temperaments. From the habitual culture of this discriminating instinct, it follows that the more intense the visceral passion of hunger, the more nicely will it select its true aliment in correspondence to the sphere of physical and passional activity in which the individual moves. The identity of essence which we have observed between the living body and the aliments which nourish it, pre-exists in the law of Passional Correspondence, " *Suum cuique tribuito.*"

What is passional correspondence ? How can I compare things so entirely different as aliments and passions ? A peach, a pear, an apple, a glass of wine, have forms, colors, odors, tastes, qualities of touch, &c., by which I distinguish them ; but what forms, colors, odors, tastes, or qualities of touch, has the passion of love, or of ambition, of paternity, or of friendship, whose principles are materialized in these their alimentary analogues ?

Have you ever heard of such a science or art as physiognomy ? If not, let me refer you to my friends, Dr. Redfield or Madame De Bonneville. They will read your character, your passions, and their habitual manifestations down to the nicest shades and eccentricities, from these very sensible qualities of form, color, touch, and sound, even without the aid of smell and taste ; the passional principle, in the physical expression ; to the wise an open secret.

Now, reasoning from the known to the unknown, from the certain to the contested, since your own consciousness establishes the existence of passional principles, reflecting or expressing themselves in the physical conformation, color, tactile surface, &c., to the senses of the physiognomist ; shall we not expect, by analogy, that form, color, tactile surface, sound, odor, taste ; all the sensible qualities which you possess, and which vary in every individual, shall be elsewhere, wherever they exist, likewise the expression and materialization of passional principles ? Perhaps so, perhaps not, you reply. Until I can enter into the peach, the pear, the apple, the glass of wine, and possess myself of their consciousness, I can obtain no proof of it, since it is only by entering into myself and possessing my own consciousness, that I know the physiognomist in the first case to have deciphered the passional principle in its physical expression.

Well you recollect the story of Mahomet and the disobedient mountain, which would not come at his bidding. Mahomet solved the difficulty by going to the mountain.

I think we have as simple a solution here, for if we cannot conveniently enter into the peach, the pear, the apple, and the glass of wine, it will be easier and quite as much to the purpose to have the peach, the pear, the apple and the glass of wine enter into us, and get at *their* consciousness, or at the passional principle pervading them, through the changes in our *own*. For the sake of brevity and simplicity, and because our coarse, uncultured appreciation seldom observes or connects with their causes the organic and passional changes which occur in us ; let us take one of these four, the wine, whose sensible qualities are more intense than those of the fruits. Can you tell me the cause or reason of that custom which prevails wherever vinous or alcoholic drinks are known, and which the spasmodic opposition of the temperance reform has rendered so conspicuous, of expressing cordiality towards friend or stranger, by inviting them to take wine or liquor with us? Why wine, fermented or alcoholic liquor, rather than tea or coffee, which are used at conversational parties; even before food in all places and at all times? Can you tell me why this custom prevails among men, in whom the passion of friendship prevails, and not among women, in whom it is comparatively feeble; or why the exit of the ladies from the dining-hall, is a signal for the wine to circulate more freely, as the bisexual relation ceases to divide the empire of the unisexual or virile passion? Can you tell me why good wine improves the temper and makes a man amiable, cordial and freespoken? Why it supplies a common platform of animal spirits or temporary intensity of the sanguine temperament in which friendship predominates, so that two men who have lived together for weeks in a boarding-house, hardly exchanging a "how d'ye do, or damn your soul, or any other sort of politeness," shall find themselves at a champagne supper in the most animated conversation, man to man, fair and free, as the over-soul will have it, careless of stupid interests, conventions, or previous acquaintance? Is not wine, then an expression in material correspondence, of the passion of friendship? The vine reveals this to every eye conversant with vegetable physiognomy, in its twining attachments and numberless tendrils which turn themselves to embrace every object in contact.

2. In its luxuriant foliage: the leaf of the plant performs its digestion and respiration, absorbing and fixing carbonic acid by day and exhaling oxygen; by night absorbing oxygen and exhaling carbonic acid. The leaf is the main organ of work, it is therefore the emblem of industry, which the passion of friendship pervades in the distributions of the passional series.

3. The vine bleeds profusely and rapidly when cut in the spring or summer—dominance of the vascular system, as in the sanguine temperament, where friendship rules.

4. The vine distributes its fruit, as well as leaves, in clusters, emblem of the group.

5. The color of the ripe fruit is either purple or violet, colors of friendship; or translucent, color of truth.

6. The vintage assembles the whole population in social groups, affording to each, attractive work suited to man, woman, and child; it attracts the gentry and rich folk, and mingles them with the country laborers.

7. Wine, which is the grape arrived at its compound maturity, develops in the organism the passional tendencies of friendship.

As we only aim here to announce general principles, one detailed illustration must suffice.

By applying these laws of passional causation and reflection of the passional cause in the organic result, we may easily satisfy ourselves that the Peach and Plum are fruits of love: amongst those which ripen in early summer, even in spring, in their native climes;

they are exquisitely delicious, aromatic and fugitive. Their trees are not long-lived, they bear early and perish early, like Eastern beauties. They feed the organism with their refined juices during the season of love, when the spiritual life needs to flow freely, unembarrassed by organic crudities.

THE PEAR is a long-lived tree, lofty and graceful, bearing late in the summer, and late in the growth of the tree, emblem of the maturer and more tardy triumphs of ambition.

A few species are preserved through the winter, as in exceptional cases, the triumphs of ambition are permanent, sustaining the winter of life, and bequeathing to children a heritage of power and honor.

The tree is extremely delicate of nurture and of fine organization.

The fruit grows singly, or along the line of the branch, but not in regular clusters.

Its form is described by a curve from the stem, similar to the hyperbole of geometricians. This ascending expansion is the type of ambition, which loses itself in the infinite.

Its fruit is gathered with difficulty from the lofty top and spreading boughs, requiring courage and firm nerves to reach them. Its flavors are highly improvable and delicious.

THE APPLE, fruit of paternity, bequeaths its fruit like a legacy to the winter months, with careful precision.

It does not assemble at its harvests whole neighborhoods like the vine, but whole families; the children gathering, the father at the cider press, and the mother storing away and preserving.

Its fruits sustain the family bond. Its gentle affections live around the hearth where the apple is the only social fruit in the climates of its growth whose harmonies of taste combine with the nuts, and are admitted at other periods than those of the regular meals.

As familism has been the Judas of the passions, basing the incoherent societies and all their physical and moral evils on its germ, the isolated household; so it is the apple which tempted man to disobey, in the myth of the Fall. It is the apple which lost Troy, by provoking the enmity of Minerva against Paris, who awarded it as a prize to the Goddess of Beauty. The apples of the Hesperides and those of Atalanta likewise occur to the classical scholar.

Fruits in general correspond to the affections, grains and fibrous food to the intellect and executive faculties. Hence the latter have entirely predominated in our diet, during the incoherent periods, when the affections have been starved, and everything has depended on executive force in resisting competition, and making good one's own against the world. Fruits come rapidly more and more into general use at this period, precursor of passional harmony, when they may form the staple of consumption.

Many obstacles inherent in the mechanism of the subversive societies, prevent the culture and consumption of fruits in abundance and perfection.

1. The tiller of the soil is for the most part a temporary tenant, removable at pleasure, when his short lease expires. He knows that all additional value which he confers upon the soil, will tempt the landlord to a proportional and even excessive raise of rent. He has enough work to sustain himself and family from month to month and year to year, without expending time and force on crops which require from four to ten years of growth before yielding any profit, and which a stranger's hand may probably reap.

2. The danger of robbery is so great in the neighborhood of cities, that the fruit cannot be left to ripen on the tree, but must be picked prematurely, to the great injury of its qualities.

It is then often kept in the markets or shops until stale and miserable before it is consumed.

3. The difficulty of transportation for want of suitable arrangements, and the imperfect connection of the interior with the great routes of travel, allows one section to suffer the privation of fruit, while it is superabundant and lies for manure in another within no great distance.

4. The general ignorance of farmers and the grossness of their tastes lead to the culture of inferior species, and by inferior methods, in the few cases in which they turn their attention to fruit.

Thus we perceive how the various facts, customs and characters of the same social period are catenated and belong to each other, how correspondence between physical and passional conditions is organized in collective arrangements, industrial and social, and how difficult it is for any individual or sect to effect a change, without a perfect knowledge of the organic movement, and especially of the laws of transitions, and the points at which they must originate. The want of this knowledge has rendered dietetic reforms hitherto superficial, limited, and transient.

The formula of a true diet is a nicely graduated correspondence to the changes and developments of our spiritual state. We ought, in a certain sense, when about to eat, to find first within us what we are going to assimilate to our bodies. The sense of taste is given us that we may thus discriminate, and it is as barbarous to eat indiscriminately, only to satisfy hunger, as it would be in music, to confound all tunes and chords in the general category of sound or noise.

It seems to be a very simple matter to know what one wants, and yet there is hardly one man in eight, who on sitting down to table at a large hotel, or first class restaurant, where he has the selection from above an hundred dishes, who will be able to dine well, to satisfy himself, to feel on arising, that he has been worthy of the opportunity; and seven out of eight will eat twice as much as is good for them before they begin to consider, and twice as much more before they have made up their minds what they really wanted.

Hunger is only the germ of discriminative taste, which for the high health and true refinement of the organism, needs to be developed by a compound discipline.

1. By well ordered and impassioned muscular and mental labors, which ally the consumption with the production of goods.

2. By the lessons in true gastronomy, practically learned in forming one's table groups, and the daily necessity of selection from amongst a thousand delicacies, according to the formula *suum cuique tribuito.* —E.

Two contrasted Emblems of Harmony, the Vine and the Date Palm.

Social science now manifests its power and unfurls its banner. Its blazon ought to indicate its pacific and organizing aim. This blazon should be composed of the emblems of harmony and of seriary labor.

Fourier has traced two pictures of the two emblems of harmony: one drawn from the Hive, the other from the analogies of the Vine. The holy Scriptures represent by the vine, the kingdom of God and his justice; terrestrial harmony. The parables of the Gospel depict the labor of humanity, under the emblem of the "vineyard of the Lord." There exists still another emblem of harmony and of justice, given by the Date Palm.

The palm is the symbol of science and of peace; Christ bore a palm branch in his hand when he entered Jerusalem. The palm also represents seriary labor; its leaf is divided into an infinity of small leaves; its side is triangular, indicating the Trinity, the first law of distribution throughout nature, explaining that seriary labor is sustained by the three distributive laws:

[1st, the *Centrifugal* or *Cabalist*, subdividing functions, allotting to each according to his preference and capacity, and engendering that rivalry which tends to the perfection of the product. 2d, *Centripetal* or *Composite*, giving social combination of adequate numbers on each branch. 3d, *Balancing* or *Oscillating*, giving alternation of functions, interlocking interests by the interchange of the members composing each group with members of other groups, which is facilitated by short sessions in labor.]—E.

The Vine is twining and flexible, it seeks for points of support. The Palm, in contrast, is erect and firm ; the fine plume which crowns it has been the model of our architecture : the first colonnades have been imitated from rows of palm trees ; and in the ancient temples, the Acanthus leaf was replaced by the plume and the bunch of dates.

Fourier, treating of the modulation of fruits in the temperate zone, considers the Grape as pivotal, and seems to indicate that there is no inverse pivot by this phrase. Pivot inverse—nothing—perhaps Cacao ? The Cacao cannot be the inverse pivot for several reasons, one of which is, that the two contrasted pivots ought to belong to two great vegetable divisions : the monocotyledons and the dicotyledons. The Cacao is of the second division as well as the Vine, and consequently cannot hold the place of inverse pivot.

The frame of an analogical classification of plants is indicated by the successive predominance of the three natural divisions in the geological strata. Thus I believe that the following division is conformable to the progressive developments of types :—

Bastard creation—without man, Acotyledons, ferns, &c.

Simple harmony—or Edenism,—predominance of Monocotyledons (palms, bananas).

Post Diluvian creation.—Dycotyledons (vines).

The Acotyledons offer in their structure and their reproduction, all the ambiguous characters which should characterize the bastard creation. The vine appears last.—(*Noah.*)

The precept of the gospel, "judge the tree by its fruits," would found the pivotal character of trees on their aptness to represent the Combined Order.

The Palm tree satisfies all conditions. It belongs to the monocotyledons, and gives, like the Vine, a bunch of golden fruits, divided into series of groups. It forms besides, in all its aspects, the harmonic contrast of the vine.

The product of the Vine gives a generous drink ; the branch of Dates offers an abundant nourishment.

The Vine requires to be much pruned ; the Palm, on the contrary, requires no assistance from man,—its stem cleans itself. Every year a new plume replaces the last, and the trunk preserves a series of scars which rise in gradations from the base to the summit, as to indicate the painful work of the ages of subversion.—(The pivotal emblems depicting not only the results of destiny but the characters of progress.)

The Vine seeks calcareous mountains, the Palm tree

sandy flats. It will be a powerful auxiliary to the industrial armies who undertake the conquest of the deserts.

The arrangement of the dates presents a series more confused than the bunch of grapes. The fruits hang at larger intervals, and the groups and sub-groups do not offer so compact a distribution. The Palm date refers to primitive harmony—to the confused series of Eden.

The degeneration from primitive harmony is indicated by the Dwarf Palm—emblem of the Savage state. It pullulates and invades cultures like the Savage Horde. You think you have destroyed it by fire and the axe, and you see it re-appear. This is because it has strong roots in the soil, living like natural rights in the savage heart. Its fruit passes in ripening from red to black : This represents the insufficiency of the labor of purgatorial societies, which despite their desire of riches, only attain poverty.

This poverty is farther characterized by the thorns which surround this fruit, useless to Man. The field of the Dwarf Palm serves as a shelter for all the heretics or truant creatures which hitherto refuse their allegiance to Man : the hare, the partridge, the jackall, &c.

But we will not trespass upon the domains of passional zoology. I wished only to plead the cause of the Palm tree, and restore it to its legitimate rank which the Cacao was disposed to usurp.

Let the Cacao remain in its place among the plants of

the Western continent, and we shall do it justice, but it must not mix itself in the family affairs of the fruits of the Old world, which has borne the burden of the six days labor in the subversive societies, and has given the chief impulsion to humanitary progress in the attainment of essential destinies.—B——Y.

THE MUSHROOM.

This plant presents one of those hieroglyphical pictures, which like the Rose and the Viper, have been easily recognized. Some summer morning after a storm, when heat and moisture have combined to hasten the processes of putrefaction, we find over the mouldering ruin of some forest tree, or in the mellow soil where refuse has been thrown, hundreds of *vegetable upstarts* in full growth, which the Sun's eye now sees for the first time. Creatures of circumstance and sphere, they send no deep and penetrating root into the soil. Owing their birth to the decay of nobler forms of life, whose fugitive elements they crudely assimilate; they are signs of corruption, and the umbrageous top which apes in form the protective majesty of the spreading Oak, only provokes derision and contempt, instead of that respect and sympathy which wait on the slow growth of toiling merit, and are commanded by the prestige which hangs around birth and blood in old-established families.

Instead of the leaf, organ of digestion and respiration, emblem of elaborating industry; the under surface of its spreading top presents a multitude of involuted pletes, in allusion to the tortuous intrigue by which the upstart has gained his position. The upper surface is smooth and bald, covering over the latter as with a mask of simplicity, which becomes vulgar assumption by the nakedness with which it obtrudes itself upon the eye. Always aping the features of excellence, its color is whitish ; not the clear brilliant white of Unity-ism, but the dead white of civilized morality, and its rounded form wears by context, the gracefulness of the pot-bellied alderman. Its aroma is rank and unpleasant, in allusion to the vulgarity of the upstart family, and its trunk and top, whether involuted or otherwise, is but a spongy tissue of cells, without any of that solid stamina, which in the valuable wood of nobler plants, results from the elaborate effort of germs developing themselves under a higher vegetative law.

The intensity of their life is all expended in rapid nutrition, as a puffed and bloated prosperity in the class represented, supplies the place of refinement and real worth of character.

The want of education is depicted in the bareness of the plant, in the absence of the leaf; and the lack of sentiment or spirituality in the absence of the flower, and in the rank odor which they exhale. Their smooth polished surface throws off the rain-drops, as truth descending from higher spheres, of which rain is the emblem (see analogy of water), glances off from minds habituated to falsehood and duplicity, without being assimilated by them.

They keep the soil beneath them dry, subsisting on

the decomposed juices of other plants or refuse matter; products of corruption.

This plant, like the class represented, is of many varieties, differing in forms, colors and properties, though all preserving very distinctly the generic type. There are some of brilliant hues, which type the chances of passional development enjoyed by those who have suddenly acquired wealth.

Some are edible, having but slightly the poisonous qualities of the class, and some have a sort of bastard efflorescence in little tufts, betokening a germ of spiritual aspiration in their typical characters.

Amongst their numerous species there is one which presents a comic allusion to the dignitaries of the church; it grows chiefly on horse-litter, and its form is that of the cardinal's hat.—EDGEWORTH.

YUCA FILAMENTOSA.

The spirit builds his house in the least flowers,—
A beautiful mansion. How the colors live,
Intricately delicate. Every night
An angel for this purpose from the heavens,
With his small urn of ivory-like hue, drops
A globular world of the purest element
In the flower's midst, feeding its tender soul
With lively inspiration. I wonder
That a man wants knowledge; is there not here
Spread in amazing wealth, a form, so rare,
A soul so inward, that with open heart
Tremulous and tender, we all must fear,
Not to see near enough, of these deep thoughts.

Often, as I looked up to the moon, I marveled to

see how calm she was in her loneliness. The correspondences between the various parts of this universe are so perfect, that the ear once accustomed to detect them, is always on the watch for an echo. And it seemed that the earth must be peculiarly grateful to the orb whose light clothes every feature of hers with beauty. Could it be that she answers with a thousand voices to each visit from the Sun, who with unsparing scrutiny reveals all her blemishes, yet never returns one word to the flood of gentleness poured upon her by the queen of night?

I was sure there must be some living hieroglyphic to indicate that class of emotions which the moon calls up. And I perceived that the all-perceiving Greeks had the same thought, for they tell us that Diana loved once, and was beloved again.

In the world of gems, the pearl and opal answered to the moon-beam, but where was the Diana-flower? Long I looked for it in vain. At last its discovery was accidental, and in the quarter where I did not expect it.

For several years I had kept in my garden two plants of the Yuca Filamentosa, and bestowed upon them every care, without being repaid by a single blossom. Last June I observed that one was preparing to flower. From that time I watched it eagerly, though vexed at the slowness with which it unfolded its buds.

A few days after, happening to look at the other, which had not by any means so favorable an exposure, I perceived flower buds on that also. I was taking my walk as usual at sunset, and as I returned, the slender crescent of the young moon greeted me, rising above a throne of clouds, clouds of pearl and opal.

Soon, in comparing the growth of my two plants, I was struck by a singular circumstance: the one which had budded first seemed to be waiting for the other, which though as I said before, least favorably situated of the two, disclosed its delicate cups with surprising energy.

At last came the night of the full moon, and they burst into flower together. That was indeed a night of long-sought melody.

The day before, looking at them just ready to bloom, I had not expected any farther pleasure from their fulfillment of their promise, except the gratification of my curiosity. The little greenish bells lay languidly against the stem; the palmetto-shaped leaves which had, as it were, burst asunder to give way to the flower-stalk, leaving their edges rough with the filaments from which the plant derives its name, looked ragged and dull in the broad day-light.

But now each little bell had erected its crest to meet the full stream of moon-light, and the dull green displayed a reverse of silvery white. The filaments seemed a robe also of silver, but soft and light as gossamer. Each feature of the plant was now lustrous and expressive in proportion to its former dimness, and the air of tender triumph with which it raised its head to the moon, as if by worship, to thank her for its all, spoke of a love, bestowed a loveliness, beyond all which I had heretofore known of beauty.

As I looked on this flower my heart swelled with emotions never known but once before—once, when I saw in woman what is most womanly—the love of a seraph shining through death. I expected to see my flower pass and melt, as she did in the celestial tenderness of her smile.

Next day I went out to look at the plants, and all their sweet glory had vanished. Dull, awkward, sallow, stood there in its loneliness, the divinity of the night before. Oh, absence !! Life was in the plant; birds sang and insects hovered around; the blue sky bent lovingly, the sun poured down nobly over it, but the friend to whom the key of its life had been given in the order of nature, had retired into silence, and the faithful heart had no language for any other.

At night the flowers were again as beautiful as before. Fate ! Let me never murmur more. There is an hour of joy for every form of being; an hour of rapture for those that wait most patiently. Queen of night!—Humble flower!—how patient were ye; the one in the loneliness of bounty—the other in the loneliness of poverty. The flower brooded on her own heart, the moon never wearied in filling her urn for those whom she could not love as children. Had the Eagle waited for her, she would have smiled on him as serenely as on the Nightingale. Admirable are the compensations of nature. As that flower in its own season imparted a dearer joy than all my lilies and roses, so does the Aloe in its concentrated bliss know all that has been diffused over the hundred summers through which it kept silent. Remember the Yuca;—wait and trust, and either the sun or moon, according to thy fidelity, will bring thee to love and to know.*

THE EPIGÆA, OR TRAILING ARBUTUS.

Emblem of the Village Girl.

Here is a little darling that loves its mother earth so well that it never can let her go, but clasps with new roots to her bosom as it creeps along, like the strawberry, plays at hide and seek in the dimples of the sod under the leaves, lays its white and rosy cheek down cunningly against its nest, and turns up its eye at you, twinkling with innocent roguishness, as if to say, "Is it possible you've been looking for me all this time?"

It is the emblem of the Village Girl, living just so close to earth, and practical home pleasures and duties, in the sweet faith of unbroken and unquestioned instincts and affections, wisely conscious or unconscious that the closer we cling to this earth of ours and all that belongs to our sphere, the more we shall get of heaven and of the sun and stars, whose influences blend with the earth at its very surface, while in deserting the sweet lowly home of the heart in ambitious ascension, and abandoning the duties that lie nearest us for speculative philosophies, we get more out of the sphere of solar light and heat, even as our balloons seem to rise toward the sun.

* Extracted from the "*Dial.*"

Under the icicled wintry boughs
All cheerily on worked she:
" In the dear God's love and tender smile
How fair is the earth to me!"
Thus merrily sang she as she walked
And musingly to herself she talked,
" In God's sweet smile and his love so free,
How dear is the earth to me!"

Day after day in her father's house
How heartily on toiled she;
O ne'er could child to a father's want
More lovingly faithful be.
Her arm was strong, and her hand was brown,
But its touch through love was soft as down.
And still she sang as sings the bee
At its summer toil, unceasingly,
In God's dear smile and his love so free,
How blessed is life and the world to me!

By Miss *.

The Epigæa incarnates the first pleasures of spring. It is a flower of faith and of friendship,—one of the flowers of the Good God, that sends a thrill of rapture through us like the innocent and charming rustic girl it depicts; that brings the first flush of spring to the lover's heart, as he stoops to extricate its fragrant white and pink garlands from under the pine tags that shelter them from biting cold March mornings.

Its leaf is rough, " for her hand is brown, though its touch through love is soft as down."

With vegetable down the plant covers itself for protection, wrapping a sort of shawl round its limbs. 'Tis a hardy and yet a tender flower,—tender as first thoughts of love that the young spring quickens in a virgin heart,—delicate as the faint blush it has caught from the maiden's cheek. Finding some of them all pale, white and cold as the snow-drift that lately had covered them, and others so joyously rose-tinged; some odorless and others fragrant; I soon perceived that it was the very dawning of love and its softening March days that they spoke of. I watched to guess by their blush and their perfume, which flowers my sweet-heart had looked at before me. Ah! those wood rambles in the dear old "North State!"

I believe the poets are right about this flower, that it makes one wish to be a child again. Here is a New England warbler in the key of Shelley's "Skylark," and the fairy who presides over the destinies of the Epigæa, and takes a pride in its fame among flowers, certainly desires me to insert them, for they have just been handed me by a friend who had no suspicion that I was writing on this subject, and here I find my own thoughts and feelings so prettily reflected, that I shall fall quite in love with them:

Darlings of the forest!
Blossoming alone
When earth's grief is sorest
For her jewels gone—
Ere the last snow-drift melts, your tender buds have blown.

Tinged with color faintly,
Like the morning sky,
Or more pale and saintly,
Wrapped in leaves ye lie,
Even as children sleep in faith's simplicity.

There the wild wood-robin
  Hymns your solitude,
And the rain comes sobbing
  Through the budding wood,
While the low south wind sighs, but dare not be more rude.

Fairest and most lonely,
  From the world apart,
Made for beauty only,
  Veiled from nature's heart,
With such unconscious grace as makes the dream of Art!

Were not mortal sorrow
  An immortal shade,
Then would I to-morrow
  Such a flower be made,
And live in the dear woods where my lost childhood played.

A. W. H.

THE HYACINTH

Is the forerunner of spring: it is the young Virgin attaining puberty; she seems closely curbed.

The leaves, in form of pointed concave sheaths or blades, press round the flower like the arguses who watch the young girl. Its colors, besides white (purity), are those of modesty, *rose;* of love, *blue;* of friendship, *violet;* such are also the distinctive traits or passional dominants of the young virgin; its perfume has something of sharpness, in symbol of the secret discontent of the young person compressed.

Its blue and violet colors are usually of a hard shade,

by analogy with the restraint which obstructs her in the development of her love and friendship.

No flower is prettier, or more graceful; more symbolic of youth in its flower.

THE TUBEROSE

Represents the emancipated woman, the courtezan of high degree. Its flower seems to dart forth and escape from between its spine-shaped leaves, as love impels the young girl to desert the paternal roof. Thus also the emblematic flower leaves the house; its intense perfume makes it necessary to take it into the free air. it is the Ninon, the Aspasia, celebrated in the world, captivating hosts of adorers.

By analogy, the tuberose diffuses her aroma afar; it surprises, it arrests many passengers, and charms the whole atmosphere. Thus the courtezan of high degree is a seductive character, who charms the multitude: she is prodigal of money at the expense of the lovers whom she impoverishes; and by analogy, the tuberose, prodigal of its perfume, leaves round its stalk traces of ravage—corollas detached, and of unpleasant aspect if they are removed. It only flowers late and in warm places.

Thus the celebrated courtezans, a Lais or a Phryne, only rise in advanced and opulent societies. Its lanceolate leaf, with sharp end, indicates a coercitive education, a yoke from which the young girl endeavors to escape; thus the stalk also seems to escape with effort from among the leaves which environ it, and which break around it, as the dogmas of education vanish before the ardent passions of a young girl disposed to free love.

The tuberose, as it blooms out, flushes with the tenderest incarnate—emblem of the sincerity of the first love in free women, who have always been carried away by their excess of sensibility.

In the early life of Bernardin de St. Pierre,* when after more than a year of happiness, such as rarely falls to the lot of mortal during the subversive periods, the Polish princess Marie M., with whom he had lived in the most intimate relations for more than a year, but with whom obstacles of family, rank, and fortune, prevented a permanent union, suddenly broke with him, and he left Poland in a state of indescribable anguish. War was at this time declared between Poland and Saxony, which suggested to him the idea of joining the Saxon army, and returning to meet his former mistress in the character of a master and conqueror. Soon after his arrival at Dresden on the 15th of April, 1765, he used to walk every evening along the banks of the Elbe, in the gardens of the Count de Bruhl, where everything spoke to his sorrow, because all bore the impress of destruction. Those magnificent gardens, where the favorite of Augustus III. had collected with royal profusion the rarest plants of the two hemispheres and the finest monuments of the arts, were now only a mass of ruins. On all sides appeared the marks of balls and bomb-shells, mutilated statues, columns

* Esquisse biographique par L. Aimé Martin.

overthrown, pavilions half consumed by fire; while amid these wrecks, attesting the madness of civilizees, arose on all sides groups of flowering plants and trees, attesting the goodness of nature. The rays of the setting sun gave a new charm to the landscape. Descending the azure in its majesty, the horizon flamed up to meet it, and it appeared suspended upon the tremulous waves of a sea of fire. Meanwhile, the parting day,

"Dies like the dolphin, which each pang imbues
With a new color, as it gasps away;
The last still loveliest, till 'tis gone, and all is gray."

And this glowing scenery of light was gradually effaced like the illusions of life.

This celestial picture gallery had a secret charm for M. de St. Pierre: perhaps Marie was looking into the same sky at these moments as himself. So distant, yet their eyes might rest on the same object, their souls might meet in the same thought, the same desire; they were not then entirely separated: doubtless she was thinking of him as he of her. Thus solitude fed his hopes, and nature recalled him to the happiness of being loved.

His solitary walks had been observed. Every evening he met a young beauty, who seemed like himself to dream and to shun the human race. There was always, however, something mysterious in her appearance, picturesque in her attire, which might awake a doubt that like Virgil's Galathea, she concealed herself on purpose to be seen. Sometimes folding her lithe form in a long white mantle, she glided among the ruins like a fugitive shade. Sometimes robed in mourning, the moonbeams revealed her still and dreaming as she leaned upon some ruined column. Again, splendidly dressed in purple and gold, she appeared with a coronet of diamonds on her brow, like one of those superior beings, who, in the times of the fairies, deigned to console poor mortals.

St. Pierre soon perceived that he was the object of her attention; his eyes involuntarily followed her, but he did not speak to her, and remained indifferent and absorbed. One evening as he rested on a bank of turf, a little page, gallantly dressed, came and sat beside him, and said, with a malicious glance, "You surely, sir, cannot be a Frenchman, for my mistress is the prettiest woman in Dresden. You see her every day, and you have not told her so. Here is a note, however, that she has sent you by me." And he presented him a paper, on which a light hand had traced these words:

"Leave grave meditations; the morning of life is made for love. I would crown you with roses, and recall you to pleasure. Beautiful and changeful as Ninon, I know secrets for all troubles. Hasten! time flies, and love passes like a bird!"

Astonished at so singular an adventure, M. de St. Pierre remained mute; the rogue of a page laughed at his embarrassment, takes his arm, and leads him off. At the garden gate a carriage receives them, crosses the city swiftly, and stops at the door of a palace adorned with a double colonnade. During this rapid course the little page kept bantering M. de St. Pierre about his sadness and love of solitude; complimented him on the happiness of being carried off by a pretty woman, and in allusion to the great Amadis of Gaul, on the Bare Rock, gave him the title of Knight of the Clouds. As for M. de St. Pierre, he sought to disguise his embarrassment under a pretense of boldness, but he was surprised at having allowed himself to be carried so far, and would have run away at once, had not shame and curiosity withheld him. Arrived at the gates of the palace, he descended under a peristyle of white marble. The page still held him by the hand, and guided him with mysterious air through a suite of magnificent apartments; but suddenly he disappears, a door opens, and at the end of the drawing-room where art had lavished its marvels, through a mist of perfumes burning in golden censers, he sees the fair unknown, bending over vases of flowers whose shades she seemed to assort.

Her long hair floated carelessly, her eyes were heaven blue, and pleasure danced in her smile. As soon as she saw M. de St. Pierre, she flew to meet him, and placing on his head, with charming grace, the crown she had just finished, said, "I keep my promise: I crown this brow with roses to banish care from it." Then she added, dropping her eyes with a slight embarrassment, that seeing him in the garden, she was touched by his sadness, and that she wanted to know why it was. This opened a charming conversation that M. de St. Pierre never could forget. The stranger added to French vivacity a shade of impassioned carelessness, as though the soul prized its gay plumage lightly, and ever and anon would poise itself o'er the unfathomed ocean of its being, on whose surface merely, float the good and evil, joy or woe, of our phenomenal experience.

Her language was of changeful love. She would pass in life like the bird that sings, like the flower that blooms. Evils are our work, she said, but joys come from the gods. We must haste to receive them as they fall from heaven. The great maxim of happiness is to rely on nothing, to glide amid objects without ever pausing, ("to skate well on surfaces.") Those who attach importance to the events of life are always unhappy. Experience tells us, "Hover over, and do not plunge deep, for you are created to enjoy, not to comprehend." Then she added, with a sunny smile: "They warn me that my beauty will pass. I know it, but *I am beautiful to-day*. I will be so to-morrow, and I know too well how quick life passes, to be anxious about a more distant future."

Uttering these words, she twined her loving arms round St. Pierre, and kindled rapture in his soul. The wreath of flowers with which she had crowned him, like that which Ogier the Dane received from the fairy Morgana, seemed to have the spell to make him forget all grief and sadness, and while it was on his head, he had no thought whatever of his former lady-love, nor of his country, nor of his relations, for all was then cast into oblivion to lead a joyous life.

Amid this pleasant converse, the page entered to announce that supper was served; then the two lovers passed into a room hung with blue satin draped with silver gauze. A troop of lightly dressed young girls covered the table with the most exquisite viands; rarest trees and flowers were grouped in a circular alcove, at the end of the hall. A globe of light, half hid behind the leaves, shone softly on this scene, like moonbeams shimmered through the tree-tops of a quiet grove.

Then stole upon the ear the distant sound of several harps, but with so mild a melody as scarce to wake the silence, like the confused murmur of happy spirits on the shores of the Elysian fields. There was in all this sphere a fairy-like enchantment that no mortal could have resisted. M. de St. Pierre did not resist. Exquisite wines, perfumes, music, the aspect of those young sylph-like beauties, that dazzling luxury, and more than all, those languishing eyes, those seductive words of the fair unknown, thrilled through his senses with voluptuous charm. The hero of an extraordinary adventure; having neither time nor will to reflect, he ceded to the fascination of so novel a position. Gallant speeches, piquant repartees followed each other rapidly; his surprise, his curiosity, the mystery surrounding all, still added to this pleasure. Yet faithful to the memory of his distant love, these raptures which restored him to its sphere, were dashed with a regret and bitterness at her rejection of him. Eight days flowed on in continued bewilderment. Surrounded by a troop of nymphs who only sought to please him, he had tried every means to know their mistress's name, but his curiosity was always excited, never satisfied. On the evening of the ninth day, the unknown, quitting her gorgeous attire, dressed herself in a simple white tunic. Never had she appeared so full of life, so voluptuous, so adorable. She overwhelmed her lover with the tenderest caresses, and, recalling to him the last lines of her note, she repeated every moment, "Hasten, time flies, and love passes like a bird." After the supper, which was delicious, she draped herself in a long veil, and entered into games which France long after learned of the beauties of the North; she revealed herself in the most graceful attitudes and contrasted expressions. She was Venus, issuing from the bath, and hiding herself under a light gauze: Helen, escaping from the palace of Menelaus with the beautiful Paris: Calypso, wandering in her island, terrible, disordered, and followed by her nymphs, uttering furious cries.

But suddenly the scene changes, the unknown regains her serenity, shakes a magic ring, and advancing in a majestic attitude: "Chevalier," she said, "a power stronger than my will obliges me to restore your liberty. I break the charm that retained you: no more cares; run to new pleasures; hasten, time flies, and love passes like a bird." Then she continued her march, and, followed by her whole cortege, left the saloon, whose doors closed after them. M. de St. Pierre expected every moment to see her reappear ; but after waiting a little while he rose to go out, when he perceived the little page coming to him with an air of sadness. He wished to question him, but the page, putting his finger on his lips, made signs to him to follow and keep silence. Arrived beneath the marble peristyle, he enters a carriage, it departs, returns to the city, stops at the gate of his own lodging, and disappears. All these events passed so rapidly, that finding himself in the chamber which he had left nine days ago, he feared for a moment that he had been the dupe of the illusions of a dream.

The next morning he called on his friend, the Count de Bellegarde, and confided to him his adventure. During the relation M. de B. changed color several times. At last he said: "I have long desired the favor which has been granted to you. I know the beauty whose conquest you have made, for there is in all Saxony but one woman that can display such magnificence. This celebrated woman was reared by the cares of the Count de Bruhl. He developed those tastes and that charming philosophy in which life appears as a festival. He designed to give her to the king, to secure a favor which had already raised him so high, but her charms proved irresistible, and his pupil became his mistress. At his death he left her treasures which she has dissipated.

"Skilful in following her master's lessons, she lives like Ninon, like Aspasia, well knowing that to deserve their glory she needs only to be as changeful. At this moment she lavishes the fortune of a Jew, young, handsome, and a millionare, whom she has preferred before the greatest lords of the court. He has been absent a month, and his sudden return is doubtless the superior power which obliged the enchantress to restore you the liberty which has put an end to your pleasures."

THE PEACH AND PLUM,

In their numerous varieties, type the two great classes into which the youth of Harmony divide, in the spontaneous expression of their character at the age of puberty. The passional principle hitherto modulating in childhood's fruits of friendship, berries, &c., now finds life's supreme mystery open before it in the problems of love and the fitting forms of its incarnation, whereby its sweet illusions and the rosy light in which it bathes our souls, may be preserved and perfected. One class borne impulsively on the tide of passion, forms its unions of contrasted sex and temperament at once, and is called the demoisellate, or corporation of recognized lovers, whose code of honor requires only decency and constancy while admitting the luxury or fruition of Love.

The other class, less ardent or more ambitious and reserved, forms the vestalate, in whose code of honor chastity is the supreme law, and so long as young persons remain in either of these corporations, being kept there by no compulsion, they are amenable to its morals, rules, and decisions.*

The Plum and Peach, analogues of these choirs, bloom together as rivals in the early spring. The Plum exhales the most exhilarating perfume, the Peach has the greater charm for the eye, a more distant and exclusively spiritual pleasure. The Plum also gives the most luscious fruit, and much earlier than the Peach, which sustains, nevertheless, in many other points, a superiority of its own. The Peach ripens later, in allusion to the delay of love in the Vestalate, whilst the Demoisellate hastens to fruition as the Plum ripens in the first summer month (at least in our Southern States).

The Plum is a hardier tree than the Peach, and grows wild much more freely, since there is a franker expression of passional instincts in the typical character. The Peach and the Vestal pay for their refinement and for their transcendent charms by many trials which may react unfavorably on the vigor of their organic and animal life; the usual tax on spiritual supremacy whenever it affects to dominate the senses and rule absolutely.

Both fruits, when ripe, contain a stone bitterly flavored with prussic acid, against which the teeth clash, warning us of the rock on which love wrecks itself—of the dangers of excess. These fruits will not be bitten

* *Vide* Universal Unity, Vol. 4.

through or devoured whole. Thus far shalt thou go, and no farther! This prussic acid indicates the passional poison which love contains in its disappointment, or the terrible effects of this passion in its counter-movement of jealousy.

You may climb the Plum tree, it is not fastidious, but dare not touch the bark of the Peach with your booted heel, for it peels away in great wounds, leaving scars. "Take thy shoes from off thy feet, for the place whereon thou standest is holy ground." It is the symbol of one of the sacred choirs of harmony.—Sacred by its devotion to the Unity and by transcendent passional uses in kindling aspiration and sustaining spiritual charm; the supremacy of soul over sense. This tree, except in a few favored natal sites, such as Southern Persia, demands the most elaborate cares;—art does more than nature for its character. Abandoned to its instincts, it degenerates to a worthless and trivial fruit, while the Plum, child of wild nature, needs little or no assistance to attain its highest perfection.

Gum, worms, leaf-devouring insects, curculio, &c., a legion of enemies, attack the Peach; while the Nectarine, which is the peach par eminence, the superlatively delicate creature, typing the supreme combination of passion with chastity, finds it almost impossible to ripen its fruits in our rude and hostile sphere. There is a little pet of the devil's called curculio, which destroys them all in the germ, and makes them drop. The ripe Plum wears a splendid livery of colors: the red, the translucent yellow, the purple, and the green; in allusion to the frank luxury of the class depicted. The Peach modulates almost entirely in white, crimson, and blood-red; the colors of unity and of ambition prevailing characteristically, while the rose-blush on its exquisite cheek is a perfect reflection of the proud, modest, impassioned vestal depicted. Nature, or as Fourier would say, the planet Mercury, parent of the Peach, has evidently been tempted to deviate in case of the Peach, from the law she had imposed on herself, not to confound analogy with identity. She sometimes gets wild with charm, and forgets whether she is fashioning a Peach or a young Girl; hence those perfect cheeks, whose form, whose blush, whose delicate down, whose soft parenchyma so luscious to the touch, invite, yet defy the lips. I have even seen peaches of the finest varieties, which had well marked lips and a chin of their own. I was peach-gatherer one summer at the North American farm, a little industrial and domestic association in Monmouth County, New Jersey, where, thanks to the care of Mr. Edward Kellogg, one may see some of the finest fruit in the country; and I well remember how I have been absolutely awe-struck before the loveliness of these vestals of Pomona, and paused instinctively, and surprised at myself, when extending my hand to pluck them whence they hung. I never felt such sentiment of respect inspired by any other fruit. Peaches of this style must be gathered with delicacy, one by one, and softly deposited in baskets; no rough shaking, or you bruise and spoil the finest fruit. The Vestal allows no liberties, and exacts an imperious etiquette in our approaches to her.

The Peach affects the elliptical form, type of mutual devotion in love, and its stone has this still more developed, with the two symmetrical halves closely united together. The tree is native in an Eden clime, and cannot be preserved in any other for more than a few years, while the Plum, a much commoner fruit, has an immense range, and more easily adapts itself to civilized climates and cultures.—EDGEWORTH.

THE TREE: TYPE OF THE SERIAL ORDER.

The tree is a systematic emblem of the movement of the passions; and first, of their two developments in subversion and harmony. Harmony is represented by the branches, whilst the roots are hieroglyphics of subversion.

The subversive ages, comprising the unhappy societies, are depicted by the roots of the tree, the part unconnected with man. The harmonic ages giving a far greater development to humanity in happy societies, are depicted by the branches above ground, rising into the air and light, and associating with man—(See Note A, table of the Social Periods). The roots creep along the earth, and hide themselves in darkness, by analogy with the eight societies of obscure limbo, of which they are the hieroglyphic, and in which the development of the passions is ignoble, creeping, compressed, and obscure. Thus men who know civilization well, give as the rule of success, the precept "mediocre et rampant."

The branches, on the contrary, escape and rise nobly toward heaven, occupying much more space than that of the roots, by analogy with the twenty-four happy periods, whose duration will immensely surpass that of the eight unhappy periods. They are adorned by a brilliant and useful foliage, emblem of the luxury which is to adorn and enrich the societies of harmony.

The first phenomenon which the structure of the tree presents is, that the combined or direct expansion, that of the branches, the portion which may be called societary with man, gives unity to the stalk or pivotal trunk, whilst the incoherent expansion, that of the roots, the portion unrelated to man, gives no unity in a counter-trunk.

The largest roots are implanted directly in the trunk, without previously connecting themselves in any under-ground trunk. This is a faithful emblem of the social movement, which gives unity in its combined order, and its twenty-four harmonic phases, and none in its incoherent order and its eight subversive phases.

The stalk or trunk, emblem of unity, eminently unites the useful and the agreeable ; it is for our buildings the most precious part of the tree, especially when continuous as in the oak and pine. It is also the great canal of circulation for the sap vessels whilst protecting the tree against shocks.

It carries the agreeable to the marvellous, the beautiful to the sublime; raising its branches high above our heads, it gives us free passage through the colonnades and vaults of the forest. Considering that all the useful and all the agreeable are combined in the harmonic portion of the tree, which shades us with its leaves, feeds us with its fruit, and protects us with its trunk, whose wood is so valuable for numberless purposes; and that the incoherent part called root, is limited to functions, necessary indeed, but equally devoid of charm and of direct and sensible use for us; we shall see in these two developments of the tree, an image of the two developments of the social movement, which unites in the highest degree the useful and the agreeable in its phases of harmony, and offers neither in its phases of subversion or societies of dark purgatory. They perform indeed a preparatory and indispensable work like that of the roots. They gather and elaborate the essential sap or materials of harmony; as great agriculture sciences and arts; which are the nutritive sap of the social mechanism: but subversive labors, like roots, have neither charm nor direct and sensible benefit. Civilized labor is all sad, obscure, and poor. It only manages to encumber its cities with beggary, and yields but a miserable pittance, comparable to that of the roots, whose wood, useless for building, and unfit even for burning decently, is abandoned to the vilest uses, though dragged from the earth with infinite toil, like the miserable harvests of the civilized laborer.

The fundamental division of movement, and the properties of its two modes of development, are then well depicted in the structure of the tree. We see that only the harmonic movement gives the unity or trunk; it gives the treasures of the branches, their wood and their fruit; it gives the charm of the flowers, foliage and shade; whilst the subversive development gives no unity, no treasures, no charm. What more faithful picture of the contrast of Harmony or Social Unity, with the state of subversion and duplicity which comprises the civilized, barbarous, patriarchal and savage societies?

These societies present in every point of view only an anti-unitary selfishness, a scale of collective and individual discord, oppression and graduated hate; which establishes the primordial dissensions among the four societies; afterwards, respective hates and discords among the nations of each society, the provinces of each state, the cities of each province, the families of each city, the members of each family; and in general result, the seven permanent plagues: Indigence, Fraud, Oppression, War, Disorders of Climates and Seasons, Generation of Diseases, Vicious Circle of Errors and Prejudices; and consequently, Corporate and Individual Selfishness; for in this chaos of disorder and misery, *Selfishness*, the antipodes of the Unitary spirit, is the only compass of safety. The prudent and experienced man is driven to selfishness, more or less restricted, protecting for his interest some relatives or confederates with whom he is in league against the social mass; despoiling and swindling by all opportunities the state and his fellow-citizens, who despoil him in return when their chance comes.

The roots of the tree depict social duplicity in all their distributions; the trunk governs them according to the Machiavelian principle, "Divide and Rule." It divides them from their very origin, without leaving to them any unitary trunk below. Thus civilized politics with its seesaws, fictitious counterpoises and contradictory policies, holds in division the principal bodies whose union would be troublesome to king and minister.

The course of these roots is tortuous, even in a free soil, like our false relations, of which they are the emblem; they are full of knots, in allusion to the obstructions with which the civilized and barbarous mechanism teems; their extremities, instead of developing themselves distinctly and openly like the last twigs and buds of the branches, subdivide into numberless and unimportant radicles and filaments, in allusion to those ant-hills of populace in rags, which are the extremes of the civilized tree and the infinitely small of social misery; a class quite opposite to the common people of Harmony, who are distinguished for their politeness and neatness, their industrial activity and their aptitude for the fine arts, as we see the extremities and small branches of the tree chiefly adorn it.

We might found upon this analogy the refutation of all civilized systems which promise unity; it is not compatible with the subversive movement; we must not attempt its establishment in the eight obsure purgatories represented by the roots of the tree, and if our system-makers sincerely wish for Unity, they declare themselves virtually the enemies of Civilization, Barbarism and Savageism. Objectors will not fail to reply to this analogy drawn from the roots; that certain plants give unity in their root and not in their trunk: the beet, carrot, parsnip and salsify are of this number. It is an unreasonable objection to argue from the exception of $\frac{1}{8}$th. This $\frac{1}{8}$th of transition being a necessary link in the chain of movement, it remains, to explain what emblems these plants give us upon the subordinate unities of the subversive order, which offers some partial unities, but no general unity.

A more specious objection is that of the external uses of the roots. Besides the work they perform for service of the tree, they are very useful in binding the soil together, preventing rains and streams from washing it away, and in sustaining a real harmony among the three elements, Air, Earth and Water; for without the resistance of these roots, declivities are wasted in dry weather by the winds which blow away their surface, then furrowed by the rain currents which penetrate their crevices: thus the soil disappears, and leaves only a bare rock, whose covering would have been preserved by a mass of roots, restraining and binding down the earth. How then, will it be asked, can the roots be an emblem of evil, and still an agent of real good, and of agreement between three elements otherwise in active war on all declivities, where the earth is carried away by the wind and the waters, unless it is sustained by the roots? This argument is refuted by the necessity of everywhere admitting exceptions. To say that the subversive order is collectively bad, is to say that it must produce $\frac{1}{8}$th of good, for every general assertion in movement supposes the $\frac{1}{8}$th of exception or transition, without which no ties would exist in the system of nature. Let us pass to the examination of the little good which the subversive order produces, and which should be depicted in the roots. The Civilized and Barbarous state is oppressive, but this oppression restrains corporations, families, and a populace whose conflicts and seditious spirit would destroy society without the intervention of some force during the state of subversion. Coercive measures are good, as they maintain the forced agreement of the Social elements, as the roots constrain the soil and currents.

The action of restrictive authority is especially needed in social transitions or epochs of administrative changes, and just so the binding of the roots is needed at the points of transition, as on the banks of streams where they hinder the current from sweeping away the masses of soil; these same roots are more needed in proportion to the steepness of a bank, and its exposure to the action of the elements. Thus by analogy, administrative repression is eminently needed in critical and troublesome circumstances, as in a famine; where the passional elements would commit otherwise frightful ravages, even as the material elements waste and lay bare most readily the steep acclivities unprovided with roots. For greater precision we may use this table:

Material Elements.	*Passional Elements.*
Fire,	Unity.
Earth,	Friendship.
Air,	Ambition.
Aroma,	Love.
Water,	Familism.

The earth without the roots, would be wasted by the air and water; and so without administrative repression, imaged by the roots, we should see the two analogues of air and water, which are ambition and family selfishness, vie with each other in trespasses against the friendly mass of the social body, living in peace under a legislation which corporate ambitions, and the family spirit so disastrous among Patriarchal Societies, where it causes as many wars as there are tribes or families; seek to overthrow. There is then an exact analogy between the Social world and the Tree. I have here investigated it generically; the analogy of each species remains to be studied.

Every tree is emblematic of a character or passional effect. The Oak represents avarice; the Pine, misanthropical virtue; the Hemlock, the man of the world; the Walnut tree, the teacher; the Orange, the generous Harmonian. But here we investigate only the picture of the social world in the general characters of the Tree.

Every general property asserted of the Tree is fully applicable to the Social mechanism. Let us add a complementary proof of this, drawn from the roots, in two pictures of subversion, one general and one partial in its character.

1st. Hieroglyphic. *Inordinate extension.* A tree which extends its roots very far, is injurious to crops, and must be excluded from cultivated lands. It impoverishes them and obstructs tillage. Thus a subversion too extensive either in duration or locality, a subversion like that of our globe, which lasts twenty ages too long, and embraces twenty times more territory than is needed for the real progress of science and arts (see Note B); such a subversion is very pernicious to the advance of industry and of wealth, which would be enormous for our globe, had it been able to limit the civilized and barbarous order to some small states like Athens, and to preserve over the extent of its surface a virginity of forest and prodigality of springs such as are still seen in America. This new continent has preserved its essential wealth, or forest furniture of its mountains and abundance of waters; [except in Virginia and other earlier settlements on the eastern coast, which have been spoiled and exhausted by the ordinary ravages of barbarism and civilization,] societies so unskilful in agriculture, that they cannot even avoid the most scandalous spoliations, for the want of embankments. (Holland comparative exception).

It is generally in those realms and climates where nature displays all her power to bless, and humbles the imagination of man by the splendor of her features and the wealth of her production, as in the valleys of the Ganges or Meschaçebe, that she teaches man in awful lessons of destruction, how her adaptations are to the race, to the united and cooperative man; and not to the individual, whose incoherent cultures and dwellings, and cunning provisions of family selfishness, she brushes like dust from the face of her violated majesty. Thou, my monarch! helpless being, her mighty voice laughs thee to scorn, in the roar of the torrent, the sweep of the deluge, the tornado's blast, the crash of the earthquake, the legions of locusts and ants, worms and bugs, blighting the hopes of the harvest; or the pitiless blaze of the Tropical Sun extending its desert domains in the heart of thy cultures! Learn then in thy anguish and thy agony, whilst thy family perish around thee, and thy wife glares with the wild eye of famine on the baby at her breast, that lesson which comfort could not teach thee; to combine thy forces in cooperation with thy brethren, to array them in the army of labor, and present thyself before the universe united by townships, provinces, states and nations, in the great Spherical harmony. Then, and not before, shalt thou be peer of the planet! Even in the winter when all is stripped and bare, Nature sadly and powerfully forcing man by his own sufferings, to observe and reflect, obtrudes upon him the type of his destiny—the Arborescent Series. The trees drop their leaves only to show us more plainly, unadorned by all that luxury of foliage, flowers and fruit, which overwhelms the beholder in sensation and sentiment, the eternal type of the Arborescent Series: the simplest unfolding of trunk into boughs, boughs into branches, and branches into twigs.

She pleads with us for her summer life, for the glorious presence of the Sun her Lord, for that culture which we owe her soils: we her harmonists, in our turn to enjoy the lavish harmonies of our joint creation. She pleads in mourning, with tears and sobs, sighing in the northern blast, hanging the blue heavens with a leaden pall of cloud, weeping on us chilling rain, wailing in the gusts that tear from the forest its last leaves, and holding her arms before us in the desolate trees—trees that have lost all but the type of Series.

EDGEWORTH.

2d. Partial emblem : the rising of bare roots above the surface. This exposure which takes place when wind, or the washing of rains, or ill-judged levelling has removed the soil which covered it, may be frequently observed in our avenues : a root now buried, may thus be next year several inches above ground, a nuisance which occasions us to stumble and fall when we walk there unheeding, or at night. What emblem is furnished by these salient roots which rise from the ground into the light of day? They represent philosophical corporations impatient of control, proclaimers of the rights of man, who have confused ideas and impracticable projects about social harmony. They commit the gross mistake of wishing to ally light with falsehood, like those roots which would rise to the part of branches, raising out of the earth their arches into light.

They depict the Societies of the Masons, the Illuminati, and others vain of their wisdom, which would play an ultra-civilized part. The roots which rise above ground and seem to affect for a short time the part of branches, cannot sustain this proud pretension, they reenter their obscurity in the earth, whence they ought never to have emerged, and whence they have only issued to become obstructions, without attaining their apparent aim.

Thus the civilized sects which would break forth to the light, attain only, after a short flourish of high pretensions, to reenter the obscurity into which the fatal essay of their doctrines replunges them ; witness those modern philosophers, who thinking to establish the rights of man, have covered with scaffolds and slaughter fields a vast empire, cast on it the disgrace of bankruptcy, and brought back military despotism whilst supposing that they led us to liberty.

I do not blame the praiseworthy efforts of genius to attain Social Harmony, but it must tend thither by the course of Unity. This can only proceed from Societary methods opposite to those of Civilization, as the trunk or Unitary part of the Tree is a product of juices directed in an opposite course to those which have given the roots.

[There is no other basis of unity than the serial organization of labor in the township ; and all political or religious or social movements which neglect this first step, allow the nutritive sap of the social Tree, to flow into the channels of incoherence, after which no possible elevation or direction of these channels can produce real unity.]

A root which rises and obstructs our path is not then vicious for seeking the light, but for seeking it in a course pernicious to man. It is the same with philosophy ; it is not guilty because it seeks the light, but for seeking it through methods evidently vicious, like those of industrial incoherence. This analogical parallel of the Social world with the general characters of the Tree, may be carried very far and extended to divisions of order and genus. We shall find in the order of the resinous Trees, a detailed picture of the subversive movement; but my present object is only to gain the reader's confidence by proving to him from the very outset that the Attraction has nothing arbitrary, since it admits no tenet which is not sustained by application to physical phenomena, and visibly inscribed in the great book of Nature.

We find pictures of the social world in all the products of her kingdoms, and preeminently in human anatomy, which represents the movement of the Passions.

In major harmony, in the body of man;

In minor harmony, in the body of woman.

We find in the Tree a much more elementary picture, better adapted for a first lesson, for a Tree depicts to us at once:

Social harmony or Societary development, in the branches;

Social Subversion or incoherent development, in the roots.

This double development of the Tree is a model of great convenience, since it unites in a single object the complete picture of Social Destiny in the harmonic and subversive Phases, whilst the human body represents only the harmonic development, divided into the male and the female, or major and minor.

The analysis of the human body in its solids and fluids, gives us indeed images of harmony a hundred fold more circumstantial than those of the Tree. They are transcendant pictures, but the beginner ought to take hold of the abridged elementary emblems, and connect many traits in one model easily embraced. The Tree is a more elementary model than the small plants; these indeed, having little development, do not present their parts so prominently to the eye, and the passional analogies discovered in them are less striking and more difficult to be seized.

In the relation of passional analogy, the Tree is a more elementary model, in proportion as its greater size presents details more sensible to the eye and mind of the beginner, and deserves in this relation to be the alphabet of our analogical studies, (though following the natural order we have plunged *in medias res*, and assigned in more amusing and fascinating allegories, to the rose, the lily and carnation; as to the harmonian vestals who welcome distinguished strangers on their spherical tour; the office of introducing us into this realm of faerie.)—E.

PROTRACTED SUBVERSION.

NOTE B.—Expressions of this character excite many objections. How, it may be asked, is such a view conciliable with the fact of organic growth in the planet and in humanity, of which this very analogy of the tree is an illustration? Is not this, others ask, an impeachment of the goodness, or wisdom, or power of God, who has either not chosen, or not known how, or not been able, to terminate our subversion at its natural period, when the industrial elements of harmony had been elaborated?

Let us beware of confusing this subject by false issues. Man may talk about Providences, general and special, and inevitable laws of organic growth, through interminable metaphysical ages, but without thereby avoiding one atom of his personal or social responsibility, or the sufferings and penalties which follow with mathematical precision on the neglect or violation of the physical and passional laws and affinities of his being; which ever since man has lived on the earth, have demanded the order of the Passional Series, and attractive Industry organized in its functions. The same stupid fatalism which causes the Turk to sit smoking in his tent, while his comrades are making it a target for their musket balls, saying "Allah's will be done, I cannot be killed before my time," pervades this day our palsied civilization; men otherwise energetic and intelligent, shrink like cowards from the social question, shutting themselves up in the vicious circle of incoherence, in some speciality, commercial or professional, truckling to customs, whose falsehood they confess; and whilst admitting the principles of Social Science, and acknowledging Harmony as our terrestrial destiny, dare to impute rashness and insanity to those who call the people to come out from this sink of misery and corruption, and conquer their inheritance. Such were the Israelites who betrayed their nation at the promised land, with false terrors of the Anakim. Can they never understand then, that in great as in small things, in the destiny of races as in the daily provision of a family, God helps those who help themselves,—that action is prayer—that the meaning and object of their life is the conquest of matter by spirit, —and that there is no power in heaven above, or in the earth beneath, capable of resisting the WILL. *That there is in fact no other power.** If they do not feel this *will* within themselves, let them at least wait in humility for its influx from the spirit world, and mean-

* Gravity is but the will or love of masses to approach each other, as cohesion is of particles, and elective affinity of atoms; an ascending progression of attractions or wills, each higher including and subordinating the lower, leads us from the mineral to the vegetable, from the vegetable to the animal, and from the animal to the spiritual realm, until, at the summit of nature, the human will rules supreme over all other natural forces. This is the scale:—

Attraction,	Gravitative, .	of masses.
	Cohesive, . .	of particles.
	Elective, . .	of atoms.
	Assimilative,	of molecules, in the formation of solid tissues, either vegetable or animal, from the fluid sap.
	Sensuous, . .	of the five senses, appreciating outward objects, and tending to luxury.
	Affectional, .	of ambition, friendship, love, and the family,—tending to social groups.
	Distributive, .	of the Centrifugal, Centripetal and Balancing tendencies, which harmonize the other attractions and elements of the social world.
	Unitary, . .	relating the individual through humanity to Deity.—EDGEWORTH.

time cease to discourage others by their croakings of impossibility.

It is as possible to conquer passional harmony as it was to conceive of it.

There are many minds which can conceive of nothing higher than guaranteeism, and the generalization of a certain comfort. Let humanity then march in its natural series of character, to guaranteeism, to simple association, and to compound association, at once, and old father Time will have no complaints of trespass on his domains, nor could he have made any 2,000 years ago, since they are all held in fee simple, within the subjective boundaries of the human soul, and all, as the *conquests* of our *machinery have already proved, convertible equations with space and with power.*

With man, because with God, one day may be as a thousand years, and a thousand years as one day.

Individually, in the relation of the soul to its organism, and socially, in the organization of attractive labor, the source of general health and well-being through the attainment of those natural functions and affinities in relation to which we exist; we have each and all, the man and the human race, the same problem to solve, and the same conquest to achieve, as God in his incarnation in the universe, and his expression through its harmonies. We may take our own time to it. As to the point of organic growth, that is a question of tendencies, not of time, except in a very general application. One man attains his growth at sixteen, another at twenty-four, and two trees of the same species may differ as many years in their periods of bearing fruit, according as their position is more or less favorable, their vital germ more or less vigorous.—EDGEWORTH.

THE MAGNOLIA OF LAKE PONCHARTRAIN.

The stars tell all their secrets to the flowers ; and if we only knew how to look around us, we should not need to look above. But youth, fixing his eyes on those distant worlds of light, promises himself to attain them, and there find the answer to all his wishes. His eye grows keen as he gazes ; a voice from the earth calls it downward, and he finds all at his feet.

I was riding on the shore of Lake Ponchartrain, musing on an old English expression which I had only lately learned to interpret. " He was fulfilled of all nobleness." Words so significant charm us long before we know their meaning. This I had now learned to interpret. Life had ripened from the green bud, and I had seen the difference wide as earth from heaven, between nobleness and the fulfillment of nobleness.

A fragrance beyond anything I had ever known came suddenly upon the air, and interrupted my meditation. I looked around me, but saw no flower from which it could proceed. It was of a full and penetrating sweetness, too keen and delicate to be cloying. Unable to trace it, I rode on, but the remembrance of it pursued me. I had a feeling that I must forever regret my loss, my want, if I did not return and find the poet of the lake, which could utter such a voice. In earlier days I might have disregarded such a feeling, but now

I have learned to prize the monitions of my nature as they deserve, and learn sometimes what is not for sale in the market place. So I turned back and rode to and fro, at the risk of abandoning the object of my ride.

I found her at last—the Queen of the South—singing to herself in her lonely bower. Such should a sovereign be, most regal when alone ; for then there is no disturbance to prevent the full consciousness of power.

Nothing at the South had affected me like the Magnolia. Sickness and sorrow which have separated me from my kind, have requited my loss by making known to me the loveliest dialect of the divine language.—We love flowers for their own sake, for their beauty's sake. We have pure intercourse with these purest creations. As we grow beautiful and pure we understand them better. I have lived with them, and with them almost alone, till I have learned to interpret the slightest signs by which they manifest their fair thoughts. There is not a flower in my native region that has not for me a tale to which every year is bringing new incidents, yet the growths of this new climate brought me new and sweet emotions, and above all others was the Magnolia a revelation.

When I first beheld her, a stately tower of verdure, each cup, an imperial vestal full displayed to the eye of day, yet guarded from the too hasty touch even of the wind, by its graceful decorums of firm, glistening, broad green leaves, I stood astonished, as might a lover of music, who, after hearing all his youth only the harp or the bugle, should be saluted on entering some vast cathedral, by the full peal of its organ.

After I had recovered from my first surprise, I became acquainted with the flower, and found all its life in harmony. Its fragrance, less enchanting than that of the rose, excited a pleasure more full of life, and which could not longer be enjoyed without satiety. Its blossoms, if plucked from their home, refused to retain their dazzling hue, but drooped and grew sallow, like princesses captive in the prison of a barbarous foe.

But there was something quite peculiar in the fragrance of this tree, so much so, that I had not at first recognized the Magnolia. Thinking it must be of a species I had never yet seen, I alighted, and leaving my horse, drew near to question it, with eyes of reverend love.

Be not surprised, replied those lips of untouched purity; stranger, who alone hast known to hear in my voice a tone more deep and full than that of my beautiful sisters; sit down and listen to my tale, nor fear that I will overpower thee by too much sweetness. I am, indeed, of the race you love, but in it I stand alone. In my family I have no sister of the heart; and though my root is the same as that of other virgins of our royal house, I bear not the same blossom, nor can I unite my voice with theirs in the forest choir. Therefore I dwell here alone, nor did I ever expect to tell the secret of my loneliness. But to all who ask there is an answer—and I speak to thee.

Indeed we have met before, as the secret memory which makes delight so tender must inform thee. The spirit that I utter, once inhabited the glory of the most glorious climates. I dwelt once in the orange tree.

Ah, said I, then I did not mistake. It is the same voice I heard in the saddest season of my youth. I stood one evening on a high terrace in another land. It was an evening whose unrivalled splendor demanded perfection in man answering to that he found in nature —a sky black blue—deep as eternity, stars of holiest hope, a breeze promising rapture in every breath. I could not long endure the discord between myself and such beauty, I retired within my window and lit the lamp. Its rays fell on an orange tree, full clad in its golden fruit and bridal blossoms. How did we talk together then, fairest friend, thou didst tell me all; and yet thou knowest that even then had I asked any part of thy dower, it would have been to bear the sweet fruit rather than the sweeter blossom. My wish had been expressed by another.

O that I were an orange tree,
That busy plant!
Then should I ever laden be,
And never want
Some fruit for him that dresseth me.

Thou didst seem to me the happiest of all spirits in wealth of nature, in fulness of utterance. How is it that I find thee now in another habitation?

How is it, man, that thou art now content that thy life bears no golden fruit? It is, I replied, that I have at last through privation, been initiated into the secret of peace. Blighted without, unable to find myself in other forms of nature, I was driven back upon the centre of my being, and there found all being. For the wise, the obedient child, from one point can draw all lines, and in one germ can read all the possible disclosures of successful life.

Even so, replied the Flower, and ever for that reason am I trying to simplify my being. How happy I was in the spirit's dower, when first I was wed, I told thee in that earlier day; I felt a shame at telling all I knew, and challenging all sympathies. I was never silent, I was never alone; I had a voice for every season, for day and night. On me the merchants counted, the bride looked to me for her garland, the nobleman for the chief ornament of his princely hall, and the poor man for his wealth. All sang my praise, all extolled my beauty, all blessed my beneficence. And for a while my heart swelled with pride and pleasure. But as years passed, my mood changed. The lonely Moon rebuked me as she hid from the wishes of man, nor would return till her due change was passed. The inaccessible Sun looked on me with the same ray as on all others. My endless profusion could not bribe him to one smile sacred to me alone. The mysterious Wind passed me by to tell its secret to the solemn Pine. And the Nightingale sang to the Rose, rather than me, though she was often silent, and buried herself yearly in the dark earth. I had no mine or thine, I belonged to all, I never could rest, I was never at *One*. Painfully I felt this want, and from every blossom sighed entreaties for some being to come and satisfy it. With every bud I implored an answer, but each bud only produced an orange. At last this feeling grew more painful and thrilled my very root. The earth trembled at the touch with a pulse so sympathetic, that ever and anon it seemed could I but retire and hide in that silent bosom for one calm winter, all would be told me, and tranquillity deep as my desire would be mine.

But the law of my being was on me, and God and nature seconded it. Ceaselessly they called on me for my beautiful gifts. They decked themselves with them, nor cared to know the saddened heart of the giver. O how cruel they seemed at last as they visited and despoiled me, yet never sought to aid me, not even paused to think that I might need their aid; yet I would not hate them. I saw it was my seeming riches that bereft me of sympathy. I saw they could not know what was hid beneath the perpetual veil of glowing life. I ceased to expect aught from them, and turned my eyes to distant stars. Could I by hoarding from the daily expenditure of my juices grow tall enough to reach those distant spheres which looked so silent and so consecrated, and there pause awhile from these weary joys of endless life, and in the lap of winter find my spring. But not so was my hope to be fulfilled. One starlight night I was looking, hoping, when a sudden breeze came up. It touched me I thought as if it were a cold white beam from the stranger worlds. The cold gained upon my heart, every blossom trembled, every leaf grew brittle, and the fruit began to seem unconnected with the stem. Soon I lost all feeling, and morning found the pride of the garden black, stiff and powerless. As the rays of the morning sun touched me, consciousness returned, and I strove to speak, but in vain. Sealed were my fountains, and all my heartbeats still. I felt that I had been that beauteous tree, but now only was—what—I knew not; yet the voices of men said, 'it is dead, cast it forth, and plant another in the costly vase.' A mystic shudder of pale joy then separated me wholly from my former abode. A moment more, and I was before the Queen and guardian of all the flowers. Of this being I cannot speak to thee in any language now possible between us. For this is a Being of another order than thine, an order whose presence thou mayst feel, nay, approach step by step, but which cannot be known till thou art it, nor seen nor spoken of till thou hast passed through it.

She heard my wish while I looked at the stars, and in the silence of fate prepared its fulfilment. Child of my most communicative hour, said she, the full pause must not follow such a burst of melody. Obey the gradations of nature, nor seek to retire at once into her utmost privity of silence. The vehemence of thy desire at once promises and forbids its gratification. Thou wert the key-stone of the arch, and bound together the circling year. Thou canst not at once become the base of the arch, the centre of the circle. Take a step inward, forget a voice, lose a power; no longer a bounteous sovereign, become a vestal priestess, and bide thy time in the Magnolia. Such is my history, friend of my earlier day. Others of my family that you have met, were formerly the religious Lily, the lovely Dahlia, the Narcissus so wrapt in self-contemplation that it could not abide the usual changes of a life. Some of these have perfume, others not, according to the habit of their earlier state, for as spirits change, they still bear some trace, a faint remainder of their latest step upwards or inwards. I still speak with somewhat of my former exuberance and over-ready tenderness to the dwellers on this shore, but each star sees me purer, of deeper thought and more capable of retirement into my own heart.

Nor shall I again detain a wanderer, luring him from afar; *nor shall I again subject myself to be questioned by an alien spirit to tell the tale of my being in words that divide it from itself.*

Farewell, stranger. I have atoned by confession; farther penance needs not, and I feel the Infinite possess me more and more. Farewell, to meet again in prayer, in destiny, in harmony, in elemental power.*

* Probably by Susan Margaret Fuller, late Countess D'Ossoli. Extracted from the "*Dial*" of January, 1841.

OTHER FLORAL ANALOGIES.

These amusing calculations of vegetable unity conduct us to the knowledge of a really useful unity, which is the passional or social. The study of analogy is a true path of flowers, and when we consider that it leads to the tripling of wealth by attainment to the societary state, what can we think of the heedlessness of naturalists who have neglected so fine a prize ?

In vain have they sought to give charm to the study of botany ; it is found that even flowers, if they are devoid of perfume as the Tulip and the Ranunculus, are incapable of fascinating women. Botany, after all is said, has hardly any interest for the fair sex. I see this confessed in the great *Dictionary of Natural History*, article *Reseda*, of which it says, " This little flower is especially sought after by women ; who prefer the poorest fragrant plants to the most beautiful which are devoid of smell. Try the experiment, presenting to a woman two bouquets, one composed of Ranunculi and Tulips, the rarest and most richly shaded, the other formed of two slips of the Heliotrope and Reseda, you shall see her choose the last without hesitation ; and while you expound to her most learnedly the beauties of your Tulips, she will be arranging the chosen flower on her bosom and bending over to enjoy its perfume."

I answer the author of this article that the lady will commit no fault according to nature, for these two bou quets flatter each but one sense. The first pleases the sight and the second the smell. It is on either side a simple material pleasure ; now simple for simple it is not surprising that women should prefer the pleasure of an active sense, as is smell, to the pleasure of a passive sense, as is sight.

But you will see women change their minds if you present to them these inodorous flowers sustained by a compound charm, by an analogical description that speaks to the senses. Let me try a lesson on the two flowers cited by our author, the Ranunculus and the Heliotrope. The Ranunculus is the emblem of etiquette—*i.e.*, of the court which is the focus of etiquette. In presenting Eliza with a bunch of thirty or forty assorted Ranunculi, make her observe in the centre the *Royal* or Pivoine. It is the only one which takes a pure scarlet hue, because the monarch, its prototype, is the only one at court whose ambition has free development. (Now scarlet is the color of ambition). It is imposing by the number of its petals, like the sovereign by the brilliancy of his retinue.

Different in form from the other Ranunculi, it is rumpled, crushed, it seems to have been pressed in the hand to spoil its roundness, it is the image of the sovereign ardently pressed by the different parties who wish to gain his favor. By imitation the Creator has ruffled the Ranunculus even in its chalice, and given to it these irregular forms, sometimes square and sometimes triangular, which, vicious in our eyes, become an additional merit by the fidelity of the pencil. The Ranunculus Pivonia and the large Carnation produce a second corolla, which escapes with effort from the centre of the first, and seems to tear itself from the cortege of the flower. It is an allegory (in the Ranunculus) on the cortege of solicitors who press the monarch and oblige him to escape from his court. It is an allegory (in the Carnation) on the escort of adorers who besiege a young beauty and oblige her to deny herself to this cloud of pursuivants.

The three other varieties of Ranunculus which represent the court have not the characters of the Pivoine. They form exactly the circle and the spheroid, figures of rapid movement. It is an emblem of their activity in their intrigues. Let us study in detail the analogies of these three species.

1st. The plumed or *jaspeé* depicts the luxury of the court in all its splendor. Nothing equals in magnificence a bouquet of the plumed Ranunculus. It paints well the *material* lustre of the court, as well by the elegant variety of its colors as by the gracious forms of the flower.

2d. The picture of the morale of the court is found in a bouquet of the frosted variety. What is the color? How can we tell, since they constantly present a duplicity of shades ; the tint is double on each petal—one color on the upper and another on the under side. Hence the flower in whatever direction it turns is of bicomposite duplicity. Opposite shades above and below—opposite shades on left to right ; besides a general vagueness of tints. They vary according to the movements of the flower and sustain the equivocal character, just as the skilful courtier knows in the oscillation of parties how to spare himself by duplicity, to take successively different masks, and to serve Jesus and Belial at the same time. This class is not therefore less agreeable, like a bouquet of the frosted Ranunculus, which despite their equivocal and undecipherable color are infinitely flattering to the eye, quite as much so as the plumed variety.

There are also found at court a class of decided characters—like Sully or L'Hopital—which the Ranunculus depicts in the third variety, the clear dark shade which does not take the pure scarlet tint reserved for the king. The said species furnishes the sternest of flowers, the black or dark Ranunculus, analogue of the virtuous statesman, who seeing human depravity in all its depth, must be the saddest of men.

These passional portraits present a lady with real incentives to the study of botany and of other natural sciences.

Otilia disdained flowers without perfume, but after this relation of the emblems of the Ranunculus, she is already reconciled with this beautiful flower. The portraits of the court, the king, and the courtiers have interested her.

"What a pity it has no fragrance!" she says. You deceive yourself, Otilia, the Ranunculus is endowed with a very sensible herbaceous perfume, and as proof of it I grasp a bunch of it and wave it a few inches from your face. Ah! She cries, what a pleasant smell.

I should never have perceived it, but how is it that when I take one alone it has no scent? Analogy requires it, for courtiers only please at court; isolated, they are ordinary men; but collectively, they create illusions and excite hopes in one who is introduced at court. Thus nature has given to the allegorical flower a collective perfume formed of aromal columns of twenty flowers assembled, a perfume without strength when it proceeds from an isolated flower.

We shall find again in the roots and leaves the same analogical justice. Do not its claws or roots obviously depict an effect of reunion, and the leaves as clearly like those of the Iris, an effect of duplicity, since they are of two sorts. I might extend this analogy to seeds and other habits.

You love the Heliotrope, Otilia;—you love close, half-miserly persons, called stingy?—No, indeed, they are no favorites of mine.—Yet you love their portrait, the Heliotrope. It is not prodigal of its charms; if it gives flowers, they are in small proportion; it imitates the parsimony of those avaricious, sharp-sighted persons who give little, but well; like the perfume and flower of the Heliotrope. The extreme economy of these individuals degenerates into meanness. Thus to the little flower of the Heliotrope we see a vegetable caterpillar succeed, enclosing its seeds.

In other respects, the work (leaf) of this plant is magnificent. Nothing can be more artistically veined than this leaf; it is emblematic of the life of those economists who pay extreme attention to affairs of industry.

Nature, which creates portraits of all the degrees of character, depicts to us in the Oak the fully developed miser, and in the Heliotrope the half-miser or economist.

Ah, I am sorry, says Otilia, I loved this little flower, but it falls in my esteem if it represents avarice.—Console yourself, Otilia, for this disclosure, this illusion that you relinquish on the Heliotrope you will recover on the Ranunculus.—It is true, you have reconciled me with this flower.—Well then, behold you at the summit of moral perfectibility, since your affections are wisely balanced between the different kinds of merit, and your mind initiated into the mysteries of analogy, of which philosophers have been talking for three thousand years without getting any notion of it.—I like to study botany in your fashion; explain to me some pretty emblems of Love.—Willingly; would you like to have a little morality with it?—Ah, morality, that is very dull, very learned.—Oh no, take courage, we will choose some emblems of marriage, of good housekeeping; pictures suitable for ladies. I will speak to you of the Iris and Reine Margarite (see pages 21 and 64), and of the *Geranium*, emblem of attractive or seriary labors, like the *Heartsease* and the *Reseda*, a picture of the future industry. It bears a perfumed leaf, representing the serial Spring of industrial charm. Its leaf is in three divisions, subdivided into two, three and two; it is the image of the Composite Series, which ought to have at least three divisions, centre and wings, each of which is subdivided into groups and sub-groups. Let us here observe the fidelity of the Creator in his pictures: to give us an actual picture of charming work, attribute of the Composite Series, the Geranium forces us to a simulation of work, we must rub its leaf in our fingers to extract the perfume, just as the composite series draws its sectaries to move hands and arms, to betake themselves to labor. We pass over the flower of the Geranium, which would draw us into long relations with the Groups.

ANALOGIES OF THE KITCHEN GARDEN.

Turnips of the republican kitchen! It is from Turnips and Cabbages that political light is about to break forth. An oracular Turnip is going to cut short the controversies on rural virtues and wisdom, whose problems the euphuist Delille has so learnedly entangled.* How eminent a post for the cherished vegetable of true sages. Could it have aspired to such glory under the banner of philosophy?

Let us then proceed to classify Turnips in political order, in a scale of analogy with the tastes and rural functions of the different classes of citizens. The family of tuberous roots; Turnips, Carrots, Salsify, Parsnips, Potatoes; is generally emblematic of rural habits, and should depict the pleasures found in the exercise of agriculture, and in accordance with the

* See his "*L'Homme des Champs.*"

views of philosophy, let us attach ourselves to the Turnips, and remark here—

1. Big Turnips, coarse country boobies:

What is Nature's opinion on the sweet pleasures which these depict in their several degrees. The big republican turnips, or coarse and thick varieties, represent the happiness of a cabin; the dainty varieties, rural happiness in the fancy cottage. The difference is enormous.

The ploughman puts his hand to the work and allies himself closely with the soil. His portrait the big Turnip behaves in the same way, and expands voluminously in size and depth.

2. The Navet Turnip, less in dimension, depicts the easy farmer, who does not go into the work quite so strong.

3. The long Raifort Turnip, rural proprietor, engages in details, which he carries through more with his mind than his body; so his portrait, the long Raifort, penetrates deep without increasing in thickness.

5. As to the Lord of the manor, he only skims over agriculture without knowing either its details or its fatigues; so the little round Turnip, his portrait, only touches the earth, not extending below the surface except by a radicle, which serves it as a tie.

This little Turnip has wrongfully usurped the suffrage of moralists; there is no plant more allied with luxury; to render it exquisite it needs beds, glass covers, frequent waterings, skilful gardeners; it is as exacting as a fashionable belle : a false brother, introducing itself at royal tables, while the big patriotic Turnips are confined to the republican kitchen of the people.

The big raw (Grahamite) Turnip may please the field laborer, but ploughing is not a favorite amusement with the landed proprietors, thus they refuse to eat these large raw Turnips, emblems of the coarser functions of industry.

This large Turnip, baked, without seasoning, is the flattest, the most insipid of all food, it must be saturated with the juices of meat and with condiments to render it tolerable, like the field laborer who becomes companionable only by much help of education and association with the refined classes. The large Turnip, after every care, is neglected on good tables, as the rustic, however brushed up, is always out of place in elegant company.

The (Navet) Turnip, emblem of the easy farmer, is already more presentable, and may, with the aid of dressings, figure in certain ragouts. Thus the character depicted may in certain cases find himself on a footing with the polished gentleman, as for instance in electoral cabals. Scipio Nasica, on the eve of an election, used to shake hands with all the Roman country voters, by the same token that he lost the consulship for a joke about their horny fists. True Frenchman, he would have sacrificed Rome for a *bon mot*. The *radis et raiforts*, portraying the agricultural character of the landed nobility or great proprietors, ought to suit their tastes, since of Turnips as of farm work, they admit only what is delicate, leaving to the rustics the rough necessities and the big Turnips of *Marcus Curius Dentatus*, roots which in their crude state are only presentable to ferocious vegetarian simplists, and would strike an epicure with panic.

It is obvious that nature in this allegorical series, laughs at rustic pleasures of low degree, inspiring distaste for their emblems, but preference for the miniature Turnips, emblems of rustic pleasures, allied with wealth and agricultural exercise in diminutive : vexatious contradictions of philosophy, which places happiness under the thatch. Nature better advised, prefers the fancy cottage or manorial palace. Thus at least opine the oracular Turnips which ally themselves with epicurean tastes only by their diminutive species, emblematic of the fortunate class which only touches agriculture and takes at its ease the inspection and the profit.

Let us now hear the oracular Carrot, emblem of rustic ambition, and depicting the learned and theoretical agronomist. Thus this root is very pivoting, pushing down deep without expanding much in size, like the scientific farmer who explores his art more than he practices it. He has the enthusiasm of science ; by analogy the Carrot takes the color of enthusiasm, orange. It is very wholesome, and is of use in affections of the chest. Thus the agronomist, a very useful person, carries remedies to the focus of industrial vices, as the Carrot cures the focus of the body—the chest. Its very abundant leaves make a useful forage, which is cut twice without injuring the plant, and serves both man and beast. Thus operates the agronomist, he is at home in the world of fashion as well as in his cultures, as the Carrot is good in confection as well as in stews and soups.

But the scientific farmer is a man in easy circumstances, and Nature in giving value to the allegorical vegetable, deposes again in favor of wealth, and proves to us that the *good* in agriculture is connected with *luxury* and not banished to the cabin.

The Parsnip (which belongs to the aromas of friendship), and the Salsify (to those of familism), would confirm by analogy the principles already stated. All these analogies would lead us too far. We can only touch one of the pivotal, the Potato, much more worthy than the Turnip of moral eulogies.

THE IRISH POTATO.

Pivotal Y *Tuber.*

Pleasing and precious hieroglyphic of agricultural groups, gives in groups its fruits, its stalks, its flowers, its leaves—groups everywhere. It is uneatable in the simple state. It must pass through the fire, the element of luxury and terrestrial image of the Sun (Planetary Pivot and representative of God), because the groups of harmony are inseparable from luxury. This condition once fulfilled, it is an inestimable vegetable. A light covering of hot ashes or a steam bath, makes of it a celestial manna which may compete with the most delicate food. Delicious even without seasonings, it seems to tell us that it obtains good without trouble by the effect which it represents, the combined labor of groups allied with luxury. It holds the pivotal rank among the tubers because it allies itself with high harmonies, political and material: with political, by its concurrence with the cereal grains which it is capable of supplying. For many years past it has been in competition with the wheat, and has made a revolution in agriculture and in politics by its title of pivotal nourishment. A rotten spot in the middle of the Potato has consigned millions of Irish to the most horrible death by famine and attendant pestilence, shaken the power of Great Britain, and determined undulations in the sea of human destinies, whose waves break at this very moment on the beach of New Holland, touching with inarticulate murmurs the heart of O'Brien and the band of hero convicts. The Irish should henceforth wear the Potato sprig instead of the Shamrock as their national emblem, for they have been martyrs to their religious adhesion to this plant. Poteen and Potatoes have presided at the wake of her glory, and the regeneration of the Potato, condemned by the philosophers with their usual sagacity, as an effete plant, whose race on the planet was run, and its life-principle exhausted; just as they say as falsely of the Irish, the Polish, and the Hungarian nationalities; the restoration of the Potato to health, betokens a good time coming for Ireland—the disease is already recognized as only local, and curable. It is true that the Potato is a native of Virginia ; but then is not America the adopted country of the Irish ? One need not be very strong in analogy to perceive that Green Erin herself is only a geographical Irish Potato at the end of a long root, trailing from the Alleghanies under the Atlantic to unite the two nations in friendship, and if hearts have aught to do with hands, then I think we are in a fair way of annexing Ireland by way of a side-dish on Uncle Sam's table, and harmonic contrast to a dish of West Indian Sweet Potatoes of the Spanish variety.

There is a reason in analogy why the Irish love Potatoes, and *poteen,* too, alas ! which is the *spirit* of the Potato, the Inverse Deity of Ireland who burns out her entrails.

The people, like the plant, is social ; its dominant passion is friendship, which it exercises in the fickle tonic of the 11th Passion, called Oscillation. It forms groups, squads, knots of boon companions with laughing dirty faces, like a flourishing lot of *praties* hanging together at the roots. They are not afraid of *soiling* their white hands, not they—heroes of spade-work, they will forever be identified with those magnificent works of Spherical Unity, our RAILROADS, where on this very day of July, 1851, while I write, hundreds of thousands of them in this great republic are delving away for the bare life till the sweat pours out through the holes in their shoes ; unconscious martyrs in that great preparatory work which Harmony will know how to value at its true desert, when it exalts to their splendid position in the social world this richly endowed victim of the British Lion, and transforms the scars and seams of conflict and repugnant toil, into the Cross and Crown of the Legion of Honor!

Analogy requires that the Potato and the Irishman should mutually reflect each other. Both rooters and diggers—the tuber has caught from the jovial habits of its human prototype a broad pleasant grin, which it always wears when well steamed, bursting open its skin on all sides. It wears the spherical form of friendship, with many eccentricities. It has only the dark and subdued colors of the soil, because it must type the dominance of material earthy necessities to which the nation is victim. Its flower is deprived of fragrance for the same reason, because the charms of passional affinity in Love are reduced to the minimum when men and women are enslaved to continual monotonous repugnant toil, with their faces bent to the earth. The colors of the flower are white and violet or purplish—unity and friendship, with a strong gusto of luxury—allusion to the regal or Tyrian purple, which came like the Irish from the shores of Phœnicia.

But it is in the spirit of Potato, the poteen itself, that the characteristic humor of the nation is developed: here you have on the one side the plant resigning its own organic life to pass through saccharine and vinous fermentations to alcoholic permanence and pivotal or unitary relations with all the vegetable and animal tissues, which like a true Inverse Deity, it at once destroys and preserves—burning out the vital principle, but defying the ravages of corruption or decomposition. And *thus* it is to alcohol, or Potatoes in the form of poteen, that the Irishman, and the American too—offers up his life, in the yearning for a greater life—to forget the slavery of care and poverty in drunken independence, and feel omnipotence and immortality course through his fired veins for one short hour. Drunkenness is the inevitable reaction and effect of passional compression. Debar man from that destiny of social happiness of which he bears within him eternally the instinct and desire, and he flies to every sort of artificial excitement, and if he cannot be nature's lord, he becomes the most abject beggar for his life. Read Martin the Foundling, that true and terrible revelation of civilized life by the Hero novelist, Eugene Sue: Read the story of Limousin the bricklayer, and it will reveal to you the fatal philosophy of drunkenness. Whisky corresponds to that social excitement of which it is the medium—and the casual awakening of this by contact of a friend or companion arouses the accumulated passional force and desire which slumbers but never dies in the Irish soul. It is only when the institutions of passional harmony raise us collectively, integrally and permanently into spiritual accords and social unities, that the Inverse Deity, the Spirit of Hell, will lose his power over the human race—until then it will continue in its effects the most fearful and fatal of prophecies. For man, destined to an immense happiness and transcendent passional harmonies, the cry of moderation is idle profanity—he cannot stop, he must go and come through at the other end. Temperance reform is a humane protest, but at last it is only a purblind palliative, a mere squirt upon a conflagration, a mockery of the almighty want of disinherited humanity. But let us return to our Potatoes. We have spoken of their political and social accords, their material ties are by a pure and simple affinity with fire, salt, and red wine, which are three pivotal agents: with this small cortege it rivals all the pomp of an Apicius. Thereupon we owe the reader a lesson in the schedule of pivotal products, the art of discovering in their affinities whether a plant is merely a note of the vegetable gamut, as the Carrot, or transition as the Turnip, or pivotal as the Beet and the Potato.

Why, it will be asked, not rather honor as pivotal tubers, those magnificent African roots, as the Yam and the Tanier; or our own Sweet Potato? These have also their glory when we treat of tropical products, but they are far from possessing the same spherical range as the Irish Potato, or even the same local values in comparison with other products.

The Irish Potato, whose accords with fire we have already noticed in culinary preparation, not only sustains with the Solar pivot of movement, organic relation common to all plants, but has some interesting elementary peculiarities. The dominance of friendship in its passional aroma is expressed in its fashion of burying its fruit in the Earth soil, element of friendship, and in the magnanimous fact of its deviation from the generic type of the Solanums, usually poisonous to man, like the Dog, from his generic family of Wolf, Fox, Jackall, &c.

The Potato is rather antipathic to water, the ele ment corresponding to familism—the family relation being too stringent and arbitrary for the developments of the Social Group. Thus a season may easily be too wet for the Potato, and cause it to rot. It does not like to be boiled, and nothing can be poorer or more sad in the culinary line than a soaked or sobby Potato.

The Sweet Potato is still more decidedly averse to water in its cooking. As to air—elementary hieroglyphic of ambition—it has the most charming accords with the Potato. If you would have it superb, you must lighten or aerate the hill where you plant it with woodpile manure and straw, so as to give a perfectly free circulation ; and a similar arrangement, only taking care besides to expel moisture, is necessary to the conservation of the root through the winter. The last accord of this tuber before it is eaten, is with steam, composite hieroglyphic of ambition, fusion of air and water by the unitary element Fire.

The accords of the Potato with the passion of Love are negative, but very useful. It has a calming influence on the genito-urinary system, which that great physician, Lallemand, of Montpelier, has used with admirable effect.

The Irish women are remarkably fresh and chaste, without a bit of prudery, which is in analogy with their favorite diet.

Why has God permitted this rival of the cereal

grains, so important to the human race, to be so long delayed? This question applies equally to many other objects, as quinine, platina, the mariner's compass, and the discovery of the Passional Series—problems of high transition, whose discussion would be here premature.

Let us stop at elementary studies, and lest the Cabbages should grow jealous of the lustre granted to the Turnips, they shall have the honors of the next season. [See second volume of Love *vs.* Marriage—to be out in 1852].—Edgeworth.

THE MELONS

Are hieroglyphics of those delicious occasional friendships which are peculiar to the luxurious sphere of warm climates, where spontaneity and fluency characterize the play of the social passions.

The emblematic plant grows and ripens rapidly, belongs only to the hot months, and atones for the limitation of its sphere by the wide range of its gastronomic harmonies. Fruit of a Solar aroma, like the chief varieties of the Grape, it sustains a subordinate position in the same scale. The pivotal notes in this vegetable gamut—Grape, Sugar Cane, Date Palm, Indian Corn, Wheat, are easily preserved for years, and even ages—modulating in the tone of immortality, and even exerting mediatorial functions towards other vegetable products, which by means of sugar and of alcohol are preserved from season to season. The subordinate notes of the scale have no such elevated functions—

they have however the aptitude for sympathizing with the pivotal aromas, as we may observe in the Melon and the Peach, which are good either alone or in combination with wine, sugar and spices, and the musk-melon even with salt also. This was a favorite fruit of Fourier's, who never could believe aught against their wholesomeness. They are only adapted however to hot climates ; he remarks that the people of Persia eat them during nine months of the year, and that we shall do the same on the return of our boreal crown and absent moons, of which five belong to the choir of the Earth, and await our advent to the harmonic periods (see the folding table), to take their place as Satellites. These problems in passional astronomy are beyond my competence, their investigation requires a thorough knowledge of three sciences—Physical Astronomy, Botany, and Music. It is not therefore from cowardice, but from honesty, that I have avoided in this work the theory and dogmas of planetary creation, confining myself to the impregnable position that vegetable and animal life collectively is manifested under certain appreciable exposures of the surface of the earth to the Solar ray, that the moon exerts very sensible modifications which we may observe in the Gramineæ, the Banana and Cocoanut, and that modern science, without undue deference to the authority or assertions of the ancient Egyptians and their judicial astrology, would do wisely to cultivate the same field of investigation, and to determine the influences of the Planets and even of the Stars of our vault on animal and vegetable physiology. Formidable problems indeed for the mere external observer and rationalist, but I imagine not insoluble to those developments of which our intuitive faculties are susceptible. Fourier employs the large insipid Muskmelon or Pompion, and the delicate Nutmeg Melon, to illustrate by contrast the state of concentrated and diffused universes. " Our universe," says he, " which is of the latter class, occupies an immense space, and the Suns of its vault are without vigor, like the meat and juice of the large Melon, which is however of the same aroma as the little Cantelope, whose juices are so exquisite. Thus of concentrated universes. Their Sidereal vault is divided into compartments ; their suns and planets acquire a lustre either igneous or shaded in colors [superior to our most splendid fireworks]. This spectacle we may enjoy at no very distant day."—EDGEWORTH.

I give merely as curious, Fourier's remarks on the cereal grains, in a few lines, which however suggestive, have somewhat unsatisfactory and dogmatic which characterizes all he has published on Passional Astronomy and Cosmogony. It is possible they be vindicated by some secret key, whose use he reserved to himself. Such reservation would have been however a criminal folly, as it compromises his scientific reputation. He ought either to have published at first the data of his astronomical classifications, or never to have assigned to them any other title than that of fantasies. They look absurd enough as they stand, but having no knowledge of music, I leave their criticism to the learned. It should be observed that Fourier never confounded these speculations with his positive "Science of Society."

THE CEREAL GRAINS.

To what stars do we owe Wheat, Rye, Oats, Barley, Maize, Millet, Buckwheat, Rice, &c.? It is clear that the Sun has been here the chief agent, for the ears of most of the cereal grains bears rays of different kinds. That of the Maize is surmounted by a radiating tuft, some, like the Buckwheat, grains of transition are devoid of it. I consider the grains as a series furnished by the Sun, the four moon-bearers, and the four neuter-stars, functioning in the scale of the first Sense (of Taste), in an order of compound diffraction. The Wheat is pivotal in Solar aroma, thus it gives a variety of seven ears in series, as emblem of universality (allusion to the seven spiritual passions, colors of the prism, &c). Barley and Rye are from the two major moon-bearers. Oats are from Saturn, they feed Saturn's animal the horse, who is half of man in regard to ambition. Rye is of the Earth's own aromas mingled, it is a grain of friendship, and has a vinous flavor. Barley and Rice are from the two minor moon-bearers. Barley is cooling, it is from Herschel. We shall see in the chapter on aromas why the creations of the planet of Love are for the most part of cold and chilling juices, though the planet is the most ardent in its aromas.

Rice is from Jupiter; it loves the water, a property

common among the plants of this planet. Thus the apple, its pivotal fruit, likes foggy countries like France. The other grains, maize, millet, buckwheat, &c., may be related to the four neuter stars ; I do not undertake to classify them. * * * *

[I now illustrate the principle of Analogy as relating to practical uses, in which Bernardin de St. Pierre has excelled. I translate from his " Harmonies of Nature."—E.]

In commencing with the solar harmony, we find trees in immediate relations with the Sun by the concentric circles of their trunks. These circles are always of the same number as the years that these trees have lived, *i.e.*, as their annual revolutions round the Sun. They are vivaceous, that is to say, they live from one year to several centuries. Finally, their genera are much more numerous in the torrid than in the temperate zones. I have brought forty-two different samples of those in the isle of France, which is hardly twelve leagues across, whilst but sixteen or seventeen genera are counted in all the forests of France. The genera of grasses, on the contrary, are more numerous in the temperate zones, and those of mosses in the frigid. Nature, which, in the torrid zone, places refreshing vinous and aromatic fruits on trees, such as the calabashes, the melons of the papayer, spices ; often causes them to grow on humble and creeping stems in our temperate climates, such as those of the Cucurbitaceæ, the Marums, the Thymes, the Basilics, and spreads their savors and perfumes even among the mosses of the North. I have seen a great many varieties of them in Finland, although I have never penetrated farther than to the 62d degree of latitude. If the Sun gives such activity to vegetation in the torrid zone, and if it impresses the annual circles of its course in the trunk of all trees over all the earth, the Moon on its side seems to extend its influence over grasses. I have remarked in the roots of those in our gardens concentric layers always in an equal number to that of the lunar months that they had been growing. This may be seen especially in those of the Carrots, the Beets, and the bulbs of Onions. It was perhaps on account of this lunar relation that the Egyptians consecrated the Onion to Isis, or the Moon, which they adored under the name of the goddess Isis. It is certain that these roots have usually seven concentric circles, *i.e.*, as many as they have been months in growing from the beginning of March, when they are sown, to the end of September, when they are gathered. In those countries where the growth of herbs lasts more than seven months, I am led to believe that their roots have more layers, and that their number equals that of the months of their year or season of growth. Thus the Onions of Egypt are remarkable for their size, as well as the roots of all the bulbous plants of Africa, and of torrid countries. These lunar periods are also remarkable in the knots of the stalks of most of the gramineæ. They are so sensible in the germination of all grasses in general, that I think I can find here an invariable character distinguishing them from trees properly so called, though they sometimes attain the height of trees in hot climates. The Bamboo of the Indies pushes forth a shoot every month (Rumphius). Francis Pyrard asserts that at the Maldives the Cocoa tree produces regularly every month a bunch of cocoas, so that it bears twelve at a time, of which the first begins to germ, the second issues from its case, the third buds, the fourth flowers, the fifth forms its fruit, and the last is ripe. The Latanier or Fan Palm, which also grows on the banks of the sea, gives a new leaf every month. The Palms, indeed, as our naturalists know, have no annual concentric layers. Their trunk is no true wood, it is but a column of fibres, whose middle encloses a sort of marrow. In distinction from trees, properly so called, it issues from the earth with the full size it is to attain. They have besides but one cotyledon, and this character is proper to them with the gramineæ alone.

The Palms are then but large grasses, in relation like them by their shoots with the course of the Moon, whilst trees, even the smallest, are related to the Sun, as we observe by their annual circles or rings in the wood. We should also rank among plants subjected immediately to the influences of the Moon, the mosses, most of which vegetate, flower, and fructify only in the winter when the Moon is in our hemisphere.

How is it with the Algæ? Naturalists who attribute to the Moon so great a sway over the ocean, cannot refuse to it some action over plants, and even over fishes. It acts sensibly upon the four orders of the animal power, and even over the human. Quadrupeds enter their love season and bring forth their young at certain lunar periods, and it is the same with the birds about laying their eggs—their bones moreover are periodically renewed, as is proved by the intermittent layers of red and white in the bones of fowls which have eaten madder at intervals. Many shells, among which is the oyster, show layers in relation with the lunar months, and whose number marks that of their life. These same lunar relations exist in the generations of insects, and finally in the catamenia of women—of these we shall speak farther upon the animal and human powers.

Although trees are in immediate harmony with the Sun by the concentric rings of the trunks; they harmonize with the Moon by the leaves or layers of their bark and by those of their fruits. I have remarked seven of these in the bark of the beech, and I think I have seen them even in each of the annual rings of trees. I also think I have distinguished them in some fruits, especially in the reinette apple. They appear when this fruit is opened obliquely, and more when it is bitten than when it is cut. Here then are lunar relations even in trees, for their vegetation and the ripening of their fruits is but seven months in our climate. Not only have all plants Soli-lunar harmonies in their roots, their stalks, their barks, and in the interior of their fruits, but they have others apparent in their petals or leaves of their flowers. These petals, like mirrors, reflect the rays of the Sun, and those of the Moon on the generative organs of the flower.

We shall first remark that the plane of most of the flowers is circular, and that their sexual parts are in the centre. Sometimes their disk is raised in hemisphere, and when it is surrounded by plain and divergent petals as in the radiata it does not ill represent the form of a star. This configuration has classed some species under the name of Aster, but it extends to most apparent flowers, which all prefer this circular form, although their stalks and leaves differ widely from it. This form is doubtless the most favorable for reflecting the rays of the Sun towards a common centre. And the same hand that has fashioned into moons, rings and other curves unknown to us, the reverberators of planets to reflect upon them the rays of the Sun, has varied for a similar end the petals of flowers. This reverberation gives flowers their luminous appearance. When I see those which enamel a meadow, and whose forms and colors are so varied, I am tempted to believe that they have some resemblance with stars which are unknown to us.

Why should Nature not have placed on the earth in flowers the images of objects that she has really placed in the heavens, since she has placed in man, transient like the flowers, the sentiment of that intelligence which governs the universe?

But how many truths he treads under foot like the flowers! He has walked over these for ages without knowing them. When Le Vaillant asserted the sexes of flowers in the school of the *Jardin des Plantes*, the celebrated Tournefort compelled him to suppress this doctrine, and never would recognize it, perhaps because he had not been the first to discover it. So modern botanists reject the harmony of petals with the Sun, of which I have adduced so many proofs in my "Studies of Nature." They virtually recognize them in the most apparent characters of flowers which they class as monopetalous and polypetalous, and the latter as radiated, lilaceous, rosaceous, papillionaceous, &c., but without intention or aim at the use of these forms. Yet Nature makes nothing in vain.

To avoid the obscurity of their systems let us be guided by the torch of day. The petals of flowers are disposed in perpendicular spikes like that of the Wheat, in radiated or plain mirrors as in the Marguerite; in spherical segments, as in the Rose; in elliptical as in the lilies, or parabolical as in the Capucine—these are their principal forms. Others, in great number, belong to unknown curves not yet calculated, but all are engendered from the sphere. It is remarkable that when the petals are radiated and in plain mirrors, the disk of the flower is in hemisphere to receive their reverberations, such are those of the Marguerite and of the Chamomile. They turn backwards or fall off when fecundation is accomplished. This disk is a little concave in the Sunflower, so it often happens that the flowers of its centre are abortive and give no seed. Its concavity may increase from its change of climate, for this plant is a native of America.

The reverberators of the Rosaceæ have a common focus, the Liliaceæ have two, the parabolic petals reflect the rays in parallels, like the vine. There are flowers in bunches, umbelliferous, like those of the Carrot, in hemispheres, in circles, and in half-circles, like those of different sorts of Clover; in divergent rays, like those of Cabbages and of most cruciform plants. If some flowers have positive relations with the Sun, others have only negative. There are labiated, which only show the extremity of their anthers, and papillionaceæ which hide them by means of an awn. Others even flower only by night—such is that of the Jalap of Peru or Belle of the Night; that of the Sad Tree of India, which opens in darkness and falls at the break of day; of the nocturnal Convolvulus also, indigenous to India. Others flower reversed, and under the shade of their leaves, such as those of the Imperial, and of many tropical plants. Linnæus perceived the relations of petals with the presence and absence of the Sun. He had observed that several opened and shut at special hours of the day, as the Taraxacum and Wild Chicory, and that most closed at nightfall. He had formed a botanical clock of them. He was within one step of perceiving that their petals were true reverberators, in harmony with the Sun, and whose duration was in inverse proportion to their action upon their sexual organs. The Rosaceæ, which are most active, because they return all the solar rays to a common centre, are also the least durable. The Rose often lasts but one day, and serves as an image to express our own quickly passing pleasures and existence. The vegetative power may then be divided relatively to the Sun into plants of the torrid, temperate and icy zones, of summer and winter, and of day and night. Hence many genera positive and negative in trees, herbs, algæ and mosses.

I have already shown some of the relations of the Banana with the necessities and varied temperaments of man. These relations seem to multiply under the eyes of the observer, and offer an example of the foresight of Nature, which exalts our sense of her kind beneficence to the confines of the marvellous. Its stalk is nine or ten feet high ; it is formed of a packet of leaves turned in cornets issuing from each other, extending to the top of the Banana tree, and forming there a splendid parasol. These leaves, of a fine satiny green, are about a foot wide and six feet long, they hang by their ends and form by their curves a charming bower impenetrable to the Sun and to the rain. As they are very supple in their freshness, the Indians make all sorts of vessels with them, to hold water and food. They thatch their cottages with them, and after drying the stalk draw a parcel of thread from it. A single one of these leaves makes a man an ample girdle, but two cover him from head to foot, behind and before. One day, walking in the Isle of France, near the sea, among the rocks marked with red and black characters, I saw two negroes, one holding a pickaxe in his hand, the other a spade, and carrying on their shoulders a bamboo, to which was fastened a long bundle enveloped in two Banana leaves. I thought at first it was a large fish they had caught, but it was the body of one of their unfortunate companions of slavery, to whom they were about to pay the last duties in this secluded spot. Thus the Banana alone gives man food, shelter, furniture, a dress and a shroud.

This is not all. This beautiful plant which in our hothouses produces its fruit only the third year, as I have seen in those of the *Jardin des Plantes* at Paris, bears under the line in the course of one year, after which the stalk that has borne it withers, but it is environed with a dozen shoots of different sizes which bear successively, so that there are always fruits, and that a new shoot appears every month like the lunar bunches of the Cocoanut. I speak here of the Bananas that grow under the line and on the bank of streams—their natural sites.

There are moreover numerous species of Banana trees of different sizes, from the height of a child to twice that of a man, and whose fruit varies from the length of the thumb to that of the arm, so that there are some for all ages. I have seen at the Isle of France dwarf Bananas, and others gigantic, originally from Madagascar, whose long and curved fruits are called oxhorns. A man can easily gather them by climbing along their stalk where the tails of the old leaves project, or by holding his wife upon his shoulders. A single one of these Bananas makes a meal; and there are Bananas of very different flavors. Though I have eaten them only at the Isle of France, which as is known is at the extremity of the southern torrid zone, I have

8

tasted there a dwarf kind that had a peculiar and very pleasant taste of saffron. The common sort called Fig Banana is unctuous, saccharine, farinaceous, and offers a flavor mingled of those of the *bon chrêtien* pear and the reinette apple. It is of the consistency of fresh butter in winter, so that no teeth are needed to bite it, and that it equally suits young children and toothless old men. It bears no apparent seeds or placenta, as if Nature had been willing to remove all that could have opposed the slightest obstacle to the nourishment of man. It is of all fruits the only one I know that enjoys this advantage. It has still others not less rare, among which is that, although only clothed by skin, it is never attacked before its perfect maturity, by insects or birds, and that its fruit gathered unripe ripens perfectly in the house, and is preserved a month in its excellence. The most finely flavored Bananas grow near the equator under the direct influence of the Sun : there are delicious species at the Moluccas, some of which have aromatic flavors of amber and canella, others of orange flower. Bananas are found throughout the torrid zone in Africa, in Asia, and the two Americas, and in the isles of their seas, and even in the most remote islands of the South Sea. The Rima, which bears the bread fruit in the island of Tahiti, is not comparable with it, though some modern philosophers present this tree as a new discovery, and as the most precious gift that Nature has made to men. It has long grown at the Moluccas, and ancient travellers have spoken of it. Besides, its uses relatively to man are quite limited.

It provides him neither with lodging, garments, nor furniture. It requires six or seven years to yield its fruit, which it gives only during eight months each year. And if it has given the model of bread in its paste, which when baked in the oven turns into crumb and crust, the Banana gives its fruits already seasoned with butter, sugar, and aromas. The Rima bears little rolls and the Banana Tree confections.

It is then with reason that the navigator Dampier, whose voyages round the world display so much intelligence, calls the Banana the king of plants to the exclusion of the Cocoanut, which sailors honor with this title, judging only of what is within their reach. He observes, that many families between the tropics live on Bananas alone. This useful and agreeable plant has so many relations with the first wants of man in the state of innocence and inexperience, that, as I have remarked, it is called in the Indies Adam's Fig Tree. It presents indeed in its large and long leaves the garments of the first man, and depicts well enough in the disposition of its fruit bunch terminated by a large violet cone which encloses the corollas of its flowers, the head and body of the tempting serpent. The Brahmins, by means of its wholesome fruits and its delicious shade, prolong their lives beyond a century. The Arabs give it the name Musa, which our naturalists have adopted, and as these people have promulgated in Europe the first elements of the sciences and arts after the Romans, I am inclined to believe that the declination of the noun Musa, which commences the rudiments of our school children, must have meant, not a muse, but the Banana tree, whose fruits would convey to their intelligence much pleasanter ideas. When I beheld it for the first time, with all its adaptations, I said to myself—Here is the true plant of man. Nature has not confined her bounty to enrich one plant with all that our necessities required in the torrid zone, but by uniting in one fruit butter, sugar, wine, flour, she has sought to entice us to make the combinations ourselves of these savors which she has placed separate and pure in plants of another genus. For this effect she has created the Palm with its species so different in their products. The Banana, which I regard as of the genus gladiolæ, only succeeds well in low bottoms, on the side of streams, sheltered from the great winds which tear its tender leaves into transverse shreds. The Palm, on the contrary, with its ligneous leaves, grows in places the most exposed to storms from the top of mountains as far as the sea shore. The Banana has only varieties which by the resemblance of their fruits are adapted to the wants of a single family. The Palm tree has species which by the diversity of their productions, can satisfy those of a whole tribe. It is true, that considering the Banana as a species of gladiola, we may connect with it in the same climate the reeds which bear different sorts of grains, and whose large leaves turned in cornets, are folded within each other, but they do not develop themselves in parasol form, and they do not present to man immediate relations with his wants. All the plants that I have named, not excepting the Palms, however magnificent their stature, appear to be of the genus gramineæ, because their seed or first shoot has but one cotyledon, their leaves being enclosed within each other, and experiencing in their growth but a simple development, whence it results that their stalk at its first appearance has the same diameter at its base as when it has attained its full height. Besides, it is without bark, and contains no true wood. The trunks of Palms are but packets of fibres without concentric circles, and whose centre is more tender than their exterior. It is quite the contrary in trees whose trunks increase in diameter each year, and whose increase is marked interiorly by circles. They are clothed with bark, the sap of their bark is at their circumference, and the hardest part in their centre. The Palms appear then to be only large plants of the genus gramineæ, and subjected like them to the influence of the Moon in pushing forth their leaves and fruits. But if trees bear within, rings in relation with the annual periods of the Sun, the Palms show their analogues externally. The first are composed year by year of concentric columns; thē second, of hollow joints placed one upon the other. Trees hide the dates of their age, Palms reveal them. Every lunar month these produce a leaf like the Latanier, or a bunch of fruit as the Cocoanut, and their whole head rises one notch. When new Palms are developed, the old, the lower which are the older ones, fall and leave upon their trunk knotty and annular notches, which serve at once as chronological marks, and as steps to climb to its summit. The Palm is supremely the Plant of the Sun. It is a gnomon that marks the hours by its shadow, the lunar months by its new leaves, the years by the old circles of its stalk. Its species, of which botanists know at least eighty, which have each several very distinct varieties, are spread around the globe in the whole torrid zone, and even more than six degrees beyond. There are doubtless many more yet unknown. Finally, there is no other plant that manifests so many soli-lunar harmonies. Those which it sustains with man are not less numerous and remarkable. The circumference of the largest has no greater girth than his arms. When he wants to climb it he makes with one of its fallen Palms a girdle for his waist, and helping himself with hands and feet by means of the rings which bear his weight, he rises to the summit to draw its wine or gather its fruit.

It is thus that in the Isle of France negroes climb with the greatest ease to the summit of Cocoanut trees. There are many well marked relations between the fruits of the Palm and several parts of the human body. As the Cocoanut trees are well enough known, I shall seek some of those human relations in the Date tree. This magnificent plant unites in itself most of the advantages of other Palms of which its species seems the prototype. It bears in its fruits a delicious nourishment, and exhaling the sweetest fragrance. Its always straight stalk, in contrast with that of the Cocoanut tree often bent by the winds, rises to at least forty feet in height. Its summit or capital is about six feet high, and is clothed with long leafy branches called palms; they are more than fifteen feet long. The leaves which adorn it, are placed obliquely or alternately, nearly like the feather of a quill. They are an inch long and two inches wide; they are pointed, woody, and resemble the blade of a dagger or the leaf of a reed. The palms which bear them are generally one hundred and twenty in number, of which eighty are inclined and horizontal, and forty perpendicular: so that they form at the top of the Palm tree a head, circular in its plane, and rising conical. From the axillæ of the upper palms grow large envelopes called elates, eight or nine in number, closely shut without and highly polished within. These elates open and there issues from each a bunch of flowers, which turn into fruits when they have been fecundated by the flowers of the male Palm. These fruits, called dates, are of the form of the mouth, disposed two by two on cords, zig-zag. Each bunch bears near two hundred of them, which are green during their growth, and golden in their mature state. Their taste is delicious when fresh, and they are preserved dry for a year, but although still very nourishing they lose their flavor, which changes to a dead sweet like that of the dried fig. All its bunches of the size of a man, loaded with their beautiful golden fruits, hang like lustres around the top of the Palm tree, surmounted by these lovely green waving palms, which form a magnificent dais above them. Finally, provident nature has strengthened the bases of the leaves and bunches of the Palm often shaken by the winds, by three or four kinds of network envelopes, strong as the fibres of hemp and similar to large yellow wads of oakum. Turtle doves often make their nests in the folds of these envelopes as in those of a drapery.

I shall not here pause to mention the productions of the Palm tree, which serve the daily wants of a multitude of people. The Arabs and the Indians feed upon its fruits—employ its hard nuts after boiling them, for the food of their camels, make vessels out of its elates, clothes with its fibre, the frame of their houses with its trunk, and their roofs with its leaves. The details of its uses as well as those of the Cocoanut, may be learned from the narratives of travellers, amongst others in François Pyrard.

ADDENDA

To the Fruit Trees of the Temperate Lone.

THE GRAPE.

Its wood is as poor as the plant is liberal, an emblem of true friendship, generous towards others and careless of itself.

[It needs to be deeply imbedded in the earth-soil, element of friendship. Vineyards superficially planted are liable to be soon exhausted. On the hill-sides, their favorite sites where these roots bind and retain the soil, the best vignerons think it labor well spent to dig holes from two to four feet deep for each Vine. It is one of the plants which most easily multiplies itself by layers. Now the sucker and the layer deviate from the minor mode of reproduction by generation, and the layer is a mode of reproduction, which does not interfere with the full vigor of industrial operation on the part of the branch, whose end is green with leaves, while its centre is immersed in the soil and striking out roots which aid those of the original stock.—E.]

It is impossible to imagine a more perfect hieroglyphic of friendship between nature and man. The plant puts forth tendrils like the Melon and other hieroglyphics of friendship, but the tendril is slight and insufficient as if to call the assistance of man, as do also its trailing branches.

[The intervention of the critical pruning knife is, I believe, carried to excess, and is an application of European hypercriticism ill borne by the luxuriant spontaneity of life in America. The black rot, so fatal to Vines in the Eastern States, has, I would suggest, something to do with excess of sap supplied from the roots, which the natural spread of the branches would distribute as Nature intended. Infinite trouble may be spared to great advantage, and a fine yield be obtained from fewer vines on the same soil, while the beauty of the culture will gain immensely by a more moderate use of the pruning knife, which destroys the equilibrium between the roots and the branches. The vine is not particular about conditions, which renders mistakes in its culture more easy; with true devotion it

8*

lavishes its efforts in the most prodigal manner, while with the modesty of generosity, that lets not the left hand know what the right hand giveth—it forbears to display ostentatiously its magnificent bunches of fruit, but conceals them with leaves, and even if you turn the branch over and expose the fruit, it soon readjusts itself. It is a peculiarity of the Vine to enrich the soil on which it grows, while other crops drain and impoverish it—its dead leaves more than compensate for its fruit abstracted.—E.]

THE CHERRY

Is the fruit of the Earth, mingling its own aromas; it is proportioned in size to this miniature cardinal planet. Hieroglyphic of friendship; it is the charm of infancy, the age of friendship; the Cherry tree, like the Jessamine, rises to a great height, though the fruit of one and the flower of the other be so inferior in size to the fruits and flowers corresponding to the three large planets. For what a difference between the Cherry, and the Pear the Apple and the Apricot, between the Jessamine and the Tuberose, the Narcissus and the Lily! But the two products of the Earth's aroma equal and even surpass in height of stalk those of the three large planets, an important fact which shows that in aromal labor (remember that both leaf and wood are emblematic of labor), the little Moon-bearer is at least equal to the three others; it sometimes surpasses them in the importance of its aromal uses, without which the Sun cannot properly modify the three others.

Childhood modulating only in two of the affectional passions, Friendship and Corporate Ambition, it seems that the Cherry, by analogy, should take the red and violet colors ; it takes the red and black, but a violet black, in symbol of friendship absorbed [in favoritism or caprice, the friendship of childhood being eminently of this class, and often unbased on any reason of merit or essential affinity of character. Thus we see children's friendships so often dissipated as they grow older, acquire new ideas and interests,] and become sensitive to differences in caste and fortune. The species called Agriotte, is that which gives a variety near the violet tinge, and depicting children of a frank, impulsive character, most susceptible of fidelity in friendship. I do not stop here to indicate the analogies of the Agriotte, Guignes, Bigarotes, Black, White, Hard, and other varieties ; the subject would lead us too far.

The series of species distinguished as :

Agriotte, Guigne, Bigarot, Black, Hard—White.

Friendship, Love, Ambition, Familism—Unity,

Would give us the analogy of the four orders of charac-

NOTE.—It should have been mentioned in the Analogy of Colors, that Black is not only the color of mourning, by the privation of colors, but also of Favoritism, by its absorption of them all ; just as White is the passional color of purity and chastity, by its *harmonic compression* of its component colors, to which it allows no other development than one simply luminous,—while at the same time it is in its positive aspect the passional reflection of Unity, by its convergence of all the colors. Thus Favoritism implies the oblivion of all special merits and attractions in a blind preference, and Unityism is forever crucifying the several passions in its works of devotion.—E.

ter of which children bear the germ. The rain renders the Cherry wormy, water being the element which corresponds to the family spirit, which is the source of the vices of infancy it should naturally vitiate the fruit emblematic of infancy.

THE PEACH

Is the vestalic hieroglyphic in. its aspect of Love. [Other plants depicting the Vestalate in other passional or industrial aspects, and even in particular effects of Love. Such are the Rose, the Hyacinth, and several of the Lilies, the Sweet Pea, the Magnolia, and even the Orange flower.—E.] The Strawberry depicts the aspect of its minor industry. The Peach bears the palm among the fruits of the scale of Love, from the Apricots of Herschel, the Plums from her eight Satellites, the Nectarine of Sappho, etc. This denotes the transcendent part which the vestal plays in Love. The vestalic corps gives to its Loves a development much more brilliant than those of the nine divisions of the Court of Love. Thus with all the functions attributed to the vestals ; they are always the most precious and fascinating, hence the products of the Solar Star Vestal, Mercury, are ineffably charming.

Those who doubt that God has attended to the

NOTE.—Water is the element of fluency and transmission. Combining with the solids of the body, it forms the blood, through whose indispensable circulation the different organs are formed, developed, and preserved, and the procreative principle transmitted from body to body in the life of the race or species. The elementary analogies are incomplete, and present interesting problems for solution.—E.

minute details of our tables and kitchens, may be convinced of it by some allegorical pictures drawn from this fruit. Representing the vestal of harmony, its form, its color, its velvet softness, faithfully portray the young beauty. The Peach has, like all the products of the Planet or quintessentiated Moon, Mercury, a transcendent charm, it likes to be allied on the table with two emblems of the vestalic functions, Sugar, emblem of Unity, and Wine, emblem of Friendship. Thus our tastes are neither arbitrary nor promiscuous, but our gastronomic appetites are regulated by passional correspondence.

The Peach, so delicate in its form and juices, has a stonier kernel than that of any of our fruits—in allusion to the difficult access of the vestal's heart.

[The clear stone varieties depict those who by the frankness, suavity and openness of their manners, create a pleasant illusion in this respect, and permit approaches only to show the repelled admirer all the more clearly the line of demarkation between Friendship and Love. The external parenchyma or meat of the Peach is quite distinct from the kernel containing its minor or reproductive sphere. It is the contribution of friendship which the vestal Peach makes to the wants or wealth of the social mass, and in which she displays all that provoking indiscriminateness of service which we remark in the character of her prototype—consenting with the same nonchalance to feed hogs as to adorn the most sumptuous table, and preserving her heart as inaccessible to the king as to the porker. Let me not be misunderstood to assign the feeding of swine to the illustrious corporation of vestals, except in a metaphorical sense—I mean only that they avoid no function of useful industry however homely and common—and make up the bed of the hired day-laborer with as much neatness as that of the rich magnate, in their functions of the harmonic dormitory.—E.]

This pretty tree is disarmed of aroma, insects devour its leaves its bark and its fruits, thus the modest young woman in civilization is assailed on all sides. Her virtue is calumniated by the libertine class and interpreted as hypocrisy ; she afterwards falls a prey in speculations of marriage to the vilest of men ; she is at last the most profaned of all beings. The Peach trees of the next creation will be completely armed with aroma, and no insect will be able to damage them. The aromas of Mercury companion with those of the Sun in utility and charm. Hence our globe will draw in the next creation prodigious benefit from this Moon, which once reentered into our gamut, will acquire an extreme vigor in her new creations.

THE PEAR,

Fruit of Saturn, is a hieroglyphic of convergent Ambition. It can offer only analogies of the sixth period, since Ambition is not convergent in Civilization.

Its pyramidal form is the emblem of the graduated corporations which it represents. Its savors, of mingled sugar and acid, depict the stimulants of Ambition and the charms which it presents in an equitable order where merit is the rule of advancement, which cannot take place in civilization.

The Pear is preeminently the fruit of display and object of the pride of cultivators. It is of all fruits the most varied, since the hieroglyphic of Ambition ought to surpass all others in the lustre and variety of the wealth it displays.

THE APPLE

Is a fruit of Jupiter, and hieroglyphic of Paternity. It is a beautiful emblem of the prudence which distinguishes enlightened fathers—the fruit of long duration, depicting the wisdom which amasses for the latter days, thus is the Apple our chief resource after other fruits are exhausted, it remains to us like the affection of a good father after the passing favors of the world.

The Apple is a curative in our diseases, and a reserve fund in destitution. It blends on our tables with the fruits of the Spring. Then indeed it is most delicious, and rivals the most beautiful presents of Flora, image of the benefits of a wise old age.

The old reinette Apple, furrowed with wrinkles, may contend for the prize with the finest fruits of the year which it has preceded. It is then a perfect emblem of paternal love, which has foreseen the wants of the child and provided for their satisfaction ; thus the Apple tree tenderly inclines its branches to hold out its fruit to man and to form natural bowers. Its juices and its meat have nothing luscious, but it is distinguished by salubrity and longevity. It is vexatious that this precious fruit should always fail to ripen near our civilized cities, on account of theft, which makes it necessary to gather everything prematurely.

TRAVESTIED VEGETABLE AROMAS, ESPECIALLY THOSE OF THE PLANET HERSCHEL.

Odi profanum vulgus et arceo. *i.e.* **My civilized friends are requested not to read this Chapter.**

LOVE, as we may often remark, possesses the singular property of divergent harmony or accord between beings—not only contrasted, but even antipathic, which is quite different. Love is the only one of the four cardinal passions which has this property, opposite the general order. It is a passion which rules all movement inversely to the rest, thus the Satellites of Herschel are in inverse orbits in a vertical instead of a horizontal plane, which leads me to believe that her neuter satellite, Sappho, is behind, in a position opposite to that of the other three.

We may recognize this harmony of antipathic aromas in different plants of Herschel's gamut, especially in the Apricot, which is her fruit of high degree; and in the Cabbage and the Cauliflower, the Opium Poppy, etc., which are also of her scale; in all the Plums which are of her Satellites; and from the Nectarine, which is of Sappho, her neuter Satellite; all these plants have flavors which seem to be transmitted by some other. The Apricot has this masked or half developed flavor as well as the Plums, yet the sweetness of these fruits, when once disengaged by fire, is very decided, and causes them to be preferred in cakes, they attain the state of preserves by simply baking them in the oven. The juice of these fruits is then composed of contradictory aromas, and it is the same with the Cabbage and Cauliflower; these are flavors travestied by the mingling of antipathic aromas; thus these plants, as well as the fruits of Herschel, are unwholesome to many temperaments.

Analogy required this contradiction in the plants of the scale of Herschel. They all depict effects of Love; but the relations of Love are entirely falsified in the four periods, Savage, Barbarous, Patriarchal and Civilized; they are always travestied by etiquette, constraint, &c.; in short, Love is among us one universal masquerade. The plants of the scale of Love, which is that of Herschel, ought, in allusion to this, to experience the same game of cross purposes in their aromas. The Truffle is another one of these travestied aromas, and like the Cabbage, mingles those which are very strong and very flat.

The Peacock, born of Herschel, participates in this contradiction by its hideous voice and legs, so coarse beside its brilliant plumage.

The scale of Love is however that which ought to give the most potent aromas, in analogy with the impressions of this passion. In the very rare cases where it has furnished a frank aroma, as in case of the Dove and the Tuberose from Herschel, or of Coffee from

Sappho, its neuter Satellite, we find flavors and perfumes of the greatest force. All the productions of this scale will be thus developed in the next creation, where Herschel will be able to furnish an undisguised aroma, in analogy with the honesty which will reign in the love relations of the eighth period. We may judge by the Dove, the Tuberose and Coffee, what delicious products the satellites of Herschel's scale will give. Her new Apricots and new Cabbages, far from being feverish and unwholesome, will give antidotes to those evils which the present creation may cause.

It is a woeful mistake to suppose that this planet, on account of its great distance from the Sun, is of an icy temperature. It is the warmest of the four Moon-bearers, and its gamut is the bést aromatized. Witness Hebe, which bears the sweetest of the eight Satellitic aromas of Herschel. She has shed this aroma on us in the Carnation. No other surpasses it in delicacy. Add this to the Tuberose, Coffee, and the Dove, if you would conceive what an assortment of delicious perfumes and exquisite meats and vegetables the ten Planets

NOTE.—The development of heat, light, and electricity, being altogether consequences of the relation of the Planetary to the Solar aromas, and by no means simple Solar effects, as we may be convinced by finding them diminish in proportion as we draw nearer to the Sun in leaving the surface of the Earth; it follows that the degrees of heat and cold, of light and darkness, with all the phenomena of electricity, will be conditioned to the aromal title or receptive quality of each Planet, which may be distributed in the inverse sense of its proximity to the Sun, or according to some law foreign to the domain of mechanical astronomy.—E.

of Herschel's scale will give us when they can operate with free aromas. The new Peacocks will have neither the repulsive cry nor hideous legs of the present species; finally, this Planet, which has treated us so shabbily in the present creation, will endow us with the greatest marvels of beauty and charm, [and this extends to the distribution of human as well as animal and vegetable types of character.—E.] Judge then of the fatuity of a generation which delays these enjoyments for the stupid pleasure of sneering at the theory of attraction until it shall have been verified by an experiment.

COMPLEMENTARY REMARKS.

The early fruits, emblems of some effect of friendship, naturally delight children. Does analogy therefore require that the other kinds of fruits should please exclusively the other ages, to wit:

LOVE—Kernel fruits: Apricot, Plum and Peach—*the adolescent age ?*

AMBITION—The Pears: conical fruit—*virile age ?*

FAMILISM—The Apples: spherical fruits—*advanced age ?*

Readers should avoid such general and hasty inductions. The theory of movement and analogy involves very numerous points of interconnection which would falsify general calculations. For example: Mercury, though [essentially] a satellite of the Earth and star of major octave, and the most precious in the scale of

NOTE.—Herschel likes the twilight—*chiaro oscura.*

friendship, operates nevertheless in the scale of Love, and there creates a kernel fruit the most beautiful of all—the Peach. And why this intervention of a star of major octave in the affairs of the minor octave? [This will be clear as the day to those familiar with the passional movement, on whose type the planetary is calculated, both materially and aromally. They will at once perceive how this corresponds to the combined intervention of the vestalic choir in the highest accords both of friendship and of love, as queens of industrial charm, and adored allies of the little Hordes, in whose works of devotion to the unity they share. They are excluded by their vow of chastity from the choirs of love, and yet they exercise supreme sway in the domain of that passion.—E.] After studying the fourth volume of the "*Universal Unity*," you will see why Mercury, who ought to be called the vestal or virgin star, ought to operate in the hyperminor scale of Love, and there create a nut fruit prettier than all those of the said gamut, composed of ten notes, which comprise in their genera all the characters of Love :

Cardinal of Love		⋈	Herschel or the Fairy.
Satellites	2	Idame,	the Faquiress.
"	3	Ariadne,	the Bacchante.
"	4	Flora,	the Galante.
"	5	Phryne,	the Bayadère.
"	6	Cleopatra,	the Coquette.
"	7	Heloise,	the Sentimental.
"	8	Penelope,	the Prude.
"	1	Hebe,	the Faithful.
Ambiguous.	K.	Sappho,	the Saphic.
Transitional,		Mercury,	the Virgin.

The Stars have given all the kernel fruits of the temperate zones. Herschel, pivot of the hyperminor scales, gives the Apricot; the seven satellites, 2d to 8th, give the Plums; Hebe the first satellite, gives the reine Claude; Sappho the Ambigu, gives the Nectarine and other varieties.

Herschel and her Moons have masked the saccharine aroma of their fruits, in analogy with our customs which make of Love an universal masquerade. This passion has not the right to show itself in free development out of the conjugal tie; it must mask itself under the flat and sneaking moralities of civilized etiquette. When the sexes meet, women must feign not to dream of anything more than pure and gentle friendship, and men to love only within these conventional proprieties, without aspiring to higher favors. Therefore Herschel who rules the aromas and fashions the emblems of Love, gives flat savors to the Cabbage and Plum, and the stars of her scale reproduce in their hieroglyphical works, these mummeries which form an effectual obstacle to the development of Love in its different characters.

Mercury has not given this masked aroma to the Peach, because it represents a type of character which is not tabooed, especially in Harmony, where a virgin is not obliged to conceal her love, her preferences, provided she be true to her statutes of virginity [spontaneously accepted, and which she is always free to break openly and honorably by passing into a different choir of characters]. Mercury and Hebe, being the two Moons of transition, give the two hieroglyphics of first Love in harmony, that of chastity and that of fruition, in the Peach and in the reine Claude Plum.

Why should these stars depart from the scale of civilized analogies to give pictures of the societary order which we have not yet attained? Why does Mercury, in the Peach and Strawberry, depict the child in societary industry and the virginity of the harmonian maidens?

[The laws of transition, whose operations we have already observed in the interconnection of friendship with love, industrial devotion with charm, and the major with the minor branches of movement, here again require that the contrasted social periods be interlocked by certain characters and their hieroglyphic animals, plants and minerals. The Vestal and the Peach, in the loveliness of their best development, are already true invasions of the periods of harmony, while in evidence of the vast number of lovely virgins that would be, but whom the hardships and falsities of the present societies crush, despoil, and make worthless and charmless, the Peach, though an exceedingly common fruit, and one that is quickly grateful for cares of culture, is for the most part as much neglected, undersized, puny, insipid, crude, gummy, wormy, pale or sickly-cheeked and forlorn, as the numerous victims of a civilized virginity.—E.]

The present creation, though adapted to portray the passions in their civilized, barbarous, patriarchal and savage aspects, must give, though in very small quantity, pictures of passions or characters in their harmonic developments, and by the same rule, the next creation which will be adapted to passional portraits of the Harmonian order must give in very small quantity the types of subversive passions. Without these transitions, movement would be disconnected and its different phases incoherent, as if Winter were entirely composed of freezing days, and Spring all of fine days. Harmony admits neither uniformity nor monotony, but requires variations and interconnections. We shall treat of this amply in a section consecrated to transitions, but not in the present work.

The Star Vestal Mercury furnishes many high transitions or pictures of harmony ; hence its products are magnificent and enchanting like the Peach, whose juices contrast with the flatness of the other fruits of the scale of Love. This is because the Peach represents a love of Harmony, while the Apricots and Plums for the most part represent the legitimate loves of civilization, in hypocritical masquerade or insipid pleasures, [the exception bearing on the comparative freedom of women in democratic countries like America, where there are in correspondence, the most splendid and delicious varieties of the Plum growing wild.—E.]

THE REINE CLAUDE PLUM

Represents the industrious young maiden among the class who, [anticipating the demoisellate of Harmony, deviate from the manners of the vestalate.]

Green is the passional color of work, thus is it the

general shade of the leaves which elaborate the sap. But where find in civilization such maidens industrious? From the moment a young girl, hitherto discreet and well disciplined, gets Love into her head, she loses the taste for work. If then youth and labor be allied, the maiden must be allowed a lover, a license which French girls of the Bourgeois class know how to secure, and in which custom sanctions them. This recognized visitor is considered as a candidate for wedlock. Young maidens thus visited are not of the grisette class who have relays of lovers, and who speculate upon them. The grisettes are depicted by the brown Plums, and the moral maidens by those of yellow hue, but the Reine Claude depicts the modest and industrious young lover. Hebe, the first Satellite, is titled for the charter of *first free love allied with labor.*

By analogy the representative Plum differs from the color of the rest. It is the best to eat raw without preparation, just as the satisfied young maiden is the least affected, the most natural, and the most healthy; the other plums being excellent only in cake, preserves, and culinary operations. This fruit, frosted over with its flour, is most beautiful to the eye, for nothing is more pleasing than the aspect of industry in lovely girls. Yet this character displays itself freely only in conditions forbidden by morality.

Hebe, though endowing the reine Claude with finer flavor than other Plums, has still been obliged somewhat to falsify and veil its aroma, since the free and modest maiden, in receiving the visits of her lover, neither confesses nor allows anything more to be known.

All the Plums, except the reine Claude, take the colors of familism, yellow, like the Apricot, portrait of the good housekeeper, or of ambition, red and brown-red ; depicting characters in whom the development of Love is checked, and taught to assume the passional tone of ambition or familism, the only passions which civilized morality encourages in young persons, [to which add, in the United States, friendship, with the violet tinge in some of our Plums.—E.]

I should have wished to suppress these passages on the planetary industry, or to present them in a special treatise, but we shall soon perceive the impossibility of isolating the Stars from a treatise on Passional Harmony or Universal Analogy. They must intervene in the first order of proofs, those of material analogy. It is only after becoming integrally at home in the theory of movement, and especially in the Passional or Pivotal movement, that the justice of these analogies can be realized.

Dry Scientifics. **The Ladies may Skip.**

PRINCIPLES OF MOVEMENT.

1. God—Active and Moving Principle.
2. Matter—Passive and Moved Principle.
3. Mathematics—Neuter and Arbitral Principle.

Distinction of Movement.

General Type: The Mathematics.

CLASSES.

⋈ Pivotal or Focal Movement.

The Passional or Social.
The Destinies, the Scale and the Mechanism of Human Societies.

Cardinal Movements.

Hypermajor—The Instinctual.
Instincts of Animals.

Hypomajor—The Organic.
Organs, form, color, flavor, and other sensible qualities of beings.

Hyperminor—The Aromal.
Affinity and communication with the Stars, aromal direction of creatures.

Hypominor—The Material.
Universal gravitation, physical mechanics.

Such is the integral formula of Movement. Our learned men are only practiced on the fifth branch, the hyperminor or material. Can we then be surprised that they know not the laws of the whole, and that they are silenced as soon as we give them a problem of causes or a question relative to the four branches of Passional, Instinctual, Organic and Aromal Movement, whose effects they have limited themselves to classify, without studying the general ties of the whole, or seeking the causes of that order which the Creator has established in them.

God, to be unitary with the other two principles, ought to coordinate all his operations on movement to the theorems of mathematics. Did he isolate himself from the neuter and arbitral principle He would fall into the vague and arbitrary; by conciliation with the mathematics, He finds the advantage of justice and economy: *justice*, since he can prove to himself and to all creatures that He is in accord with a rule of eternal justice; economy, since the observance of the mathematical laws gives him the means of obtaining in all movement the greatest results with the least cost of means.

Sustained by this double advantage, God has chosen the mathematical principle as general type of all movements, classed in five divisions, of which one, that of the Passional or Social, is superior to the four others. The passions are the very essence of God, and as the active or moving principle, God, is more noble than matter, the passive and moved principle, the most noble of the five movements is that which partakes most of the essence of God. This is the Passional or

Social. The others are subject to progressive degradation, and lose by degrees their alliance with the passions. It is very strong in the instinctual movement, and very weak in the material movement, which for this reason occupies the last rank as least partaking of the divine or passional essence.

If the mathematics are the mould or type of the movement; its pivot or focus is God, the moving principle, to whom all must be coordinate. Consequently the four movements, Instinctual, Organic, Aromal and Material, should be coordinated to the Passional, which is the essence of God, allied with mathematical justice. The passions are the mathematics animated, of which we shall *be made conscious* in the treatise on their harmony by contrasted series, which form the general mode of development and of relations in the Societary state.

The four cardinal movements being coordinate to the passional, every effect of these movements must be a picture of the effects of the passional and of the properties of the passions. Thus to study the integral system of the five movements, to determine the causes and the ends of the order that is seen to reign in them, we must study the system of the passional to which all is related, and of which all created objects are hieroglyphics, and in studying movement by the analysis and synthesis of passional attraction, we must recur to the mathematical laws, since they are the type of the whole system, even of the passional, to which the four others are adapted. The human mind having consulted and followed the mathematical laws in studying the fifth branch of movement, the hypominor or material, it ought to have succeeded, and has fully succeeded, especially since the time of Newton. For the same reason it could but miscarry on the four branches, of which it has only made an abstract sophistical study, and often only a criticism instead of a study.

[Philosophers, moralists and theologians have contented themselves with slandering the work of God in human passions, and devising means of compressing or extirpating them instead of seeking the aims and ends of the passional movement by a regular analysis and synthesis. Hence civilized science has been left without a clue in the organic movement, of which medicine, the principal branch, has been left a chaos of empiricism until Hahnemann and his disciples condescended to study the relations of drugs with the soul or passional movement,as well as with the body. Hence Zoology, which pretends to be conversant with instinctual movement as well as botany, a branch of the organic, have been hitherto dry and unattractive to most minds, because disinherited of that beauty and interest which is reflected on them by their connection with the Social or passional movement.—E.] Our successes have been limited to the material branch, the only one of which we have made a regular and mathematical study. A deplorable effect of this course, is to *engulf* genius.

In commencing its studies on the fifth branch of movement, where they should terminate, genius has fallen into a scientific abyss, in which it finds itself isolated from the other branches of the system of nature.

Thus despite its gigantic progress in the theory of material movement, it does not acquire the least notion of the others, especially in the social movement, and of the aim of those *passions* whose enigma is more than ever the despair of genius.

When we find ourselves in a blind alley or *cul de sac*, there is nothing left but to retrace our steps. The human mind ought to be now well convinced that knowledge of the laws of material movement does not lead to the knowledge of the other four branches of laws, nor of the general causes, which are the relation or hieroglyphical unity of the four cardinal movements with the passional. It is then this that we must study, in order to penetrate the laws of the other four simultaneously.

Without the knowledge of the integral system, the study of Nature is but an immense labyrinth to us, nor can we resolve any problem of causes such as these.

In the Material ; Why has God given a satellite to the Earth and not to Venus, which is of equal size or nearly so?

In the Aromal ; Why has God given perfume to the Rose and not to the Tulip?

In the Organic ; Why has God willed that three of tne petals of the flower called Pansy should surmount the two others, and join to the Violet the yellow, which is refused to the two lower petals?

In the Instinctual ; Why has he given to the Bee

an industry doubly productive, in wax and in honey, and to the Wasp an industry completely unproductive?

These dispositions, as well as all order established in Nature, have for their cause hieroglyphical unity, or the necessity of representing in the four cardinal movements the effects of the passional or pivotal, to which all is coordinated.

Providence has wisely designed that our studies should begin with the easiest and the most necessary branch, by the study of man, or analytic and synthetic calculation of passional attractions or repulsions: by commencing here we should have had the double advantage:

1st. Of discovering the unitary mechanism assigned by God to human societies, the social code of Harmony which He has composed for the equilibrium of the passions in the three spheres of relations, domestic, industrial and administrative.

2d. Of advancing rapidly and in less than one century in the knowledge of the four cardinal movements, which are coordinated to the passional, which is itself geometrical.

Twenty-five centuries ago we might then have penetrated the pretended mysteries of nature if we had adopted the direct and easy course of commencing by the study of man or of passional attraction. The Greek sophists, whose method we still pursue, adopted an opposite policy. They only insulted Attraction in place of studying it by analysis and synthesis. Thus they missed the theory of the passional movement, path of entrance to the four others, while the theory of the material movement leads to nothing and becomes a blind path for science, bewildering the human mind, which is unfit for all progress in the integral laws of movement until it shall have turned back, changed its course, and as Bacon says, reformed its understanding, forgotten all that it has learned of the uncertain science—[Theology, Morals, Philosophy and Political Economy] all absorbed in insulting and repressing attraction instead of studying its aim, which is the formation of the passional series and the unitary harmony of the three functions, domestic, industrial and administrative.

The analyses of modern philosophers reduce our studies to three principal branches : God, Man and the Universe. Let us show that philosophy has chosen to study neither Man, nor God, nor the Universe.

As to Man, I have elsewhere, " New Industrial World " and " Universal Unity," made known the aim towards which he should tend, the discovery of the social domestic and industrial destiny, the organization of the *integral soul*, which can only be developed through association and the combined development of the 810 primordial types of character.

Their combination produces the *complete passional man* or general concert of passions. This knowledge was the first to which we should have aspired, since to what purpose our progress in the fixed sciences while we are ignorant of the road to collective riches, happiness, and passional harmony?

God had wisely desired that our studies should begin at the most urgent branch, that of domestic association, whence spring riches, internal unity and happiness.

Hence it is easy to rise higher, to pass to external industrial unity, by the serial association of towns in the system of truthful and guaranteed commerce, then to spherical unity by the federal association of all the administrations of the globe. Such are the three primordial scales of the social mechanism, or science of man and destiny of his passions. Once initiated into this science, the human mind will march with giant steps in the study of the four cardinal movements, which are only hieroglyphical applications to the passional or pivotal movement.

Thus the study of man would have conducted us to the study of the Universe. When we know man and the universe theoretically, we know in the same manner the properties and character of God [with whom we are at the same time brought into a more interior consciousness through the perfections which our souls and bodies acquire in the social order adapted to them].

The universe, *circulus œterni motus*, is a circle which the student may traverse either in a direct or an inverse direction. The human mind has followed the inverse course. Instead of entering on its career by the point easiest of access, the study of man, so urgent in respect to happiness, it has chosen to commence by that of the whole universe. This was choosing one infinitely long, it was going backwards and traversing the entire circle to get from one point to the point lying nearest; but we could still have attained the end by this route had we not deviated from the track to cast ourselves into the arbitrary confusion of mere brain cobwebs of philosophy, having no relation whatever to practical life, to any fact or being, however humble in the whole universe.

To commence our studies by that of man, we needed a class of scientific men which has never existed, that of metaphysicians. Many arrogate this title, and not one has the right to it, for if metaphysics has for its principal object the study of man, that is to say, the analytic and synthetic calculation of personal attractions and repulsions, can we admit to the rank of metaphysicians those who, neglecting the essential, have attached themselves like our ideologues to the bark of the problem [as to silly and useless definitions of the cognitions of the perceptions of sensation]?

In commencing by the study of the universe, by embracing the whole instead of the initial point, there was need of the concurrence of all the learned classes united. They have never combined. Each has isolated itself from the rest, and especially from the philosophical class to which the study of the passions fell, a study which it conducted in opposition to common sense, since one of their leading classes, the moralists, pretends to annihilate the passions, to change this and repress that. Now it is not studying Nature to try to contradict, to annihilate it. Thus have the philosophers attained no knowledge of passional or hominal nature.

[The honest course has actually been opened of late years by Parent Du Chatelet and others, who devote themselves to the acquisition of Social statistics in the great capitals of Europe. It is true that the classes in power have as yet done little or nothing for the radical cure of the evils thus evidenced, but here at least is something that looks like the real study of man.—E.]

Geometricians and astronomers, proud of some success in the calculations of material effects, have triumphed as if the secret of nature had been surprised, as if the theory of causes and ends had been explored. Yet so far from being advanced in physical science, they cannot answer the least question upon causes, and if you ask why Herschel, sixteen times smaller than Jupiter, bears a double number of Moons, none of them can give the solution of the problem, which would be a trifle if they understood the theory of causes.

It has been already recognized that the material, fifth branch, is entirely coordinated to the mathematics.

A similar observation has been made on the organic movement; the structure of an animal body, its bony skeleton, the play of the muscles and viscera, all this mechanism rigorously follows the mathematical laws. It is the same with the instinctual movement of animals. The bee, the wasp, the beaver, the spider, even caterpillars, in their labors, are all geometricians by instinct, and never depart from the mathematical laws. Now these creatures being moved directly by God, obeying brute attraction, it becomes evident that God rules by mathematical laws the instinctual movement as well as the organic and material. Here are already three of the cardinal movements subjected to the same law. In awaiting a more extended knowledge of the aromal, I observe that our operation on the gases, on light and electricity, are successful only so far as we follow their mathematical laws. We also see aromas direct the stars and their conjugations very mathematically in the play of their affinities. Behold then in the four cardinal movements an accord of the three principles of the universe, of God with the mathematics, whose laws he observes in the direction and modification of matter. In virtue of Unity, the pivotal or passional movement must be submitted to the same system, otherwise we can conceive of no unity in the universe, nor in the Spirit of God. But if we observe that the instinctual movement which is nearest to the passional is mathematically directed as well as the three others, it is a pressing indication of the unity of the passional with the system of the four cardinal movements. How can instincts which are almost identical with passions be coordinated to mathematical laws without their also applying to passions? And if we perceive that such divergence would cause God to fall into duplicity of system, it becomes indubitable even before knowing the laws of passional movement that they are mathematical.

Such are the first inductions that the human mind would have drawn, had it investigated the task which it assumed, the study of the universe or totality of movement and integral sum of the five branches. It would have concluded at once that the system of God on the mechanism of the passions must be mathematical.*

Henceforth we should absolve from ridicule all that is mathematical, and especially passional attraction, whose study the philosophers derided as frivolous. Can there be anything frivolous in an agent which directs mathematically the four cardinal movements (above stated), and which ought to direct the passional in the same manner? We conclude that whether amusing or otherwise, passional attraction should become the

* For the scope of this word, *Mathematical*, as applied to the vital forces, see my "*Passional Hygiene*," (page 70) published by Radde, No. 322 Broadway. "The relation of the passions with the rules of arithmetic," in my work on "*Homœopathy*," page 36, and consecutive. See also Articles "Passional Arithmetic" and "Passional Geometry," in my translation of Toussenel's "*Passional Zoology*," now in press.

By the term God, Fourier here means the complex or sum total of creative and conservative forces, without here discussing the question whether they are or are not resumed in a monad, dyad, triad, tetrad or polyad, either discrete from what we designate as Nature, or concrete with it. He leaves aside all these silly, theological, metaphysical, vain, empty, windy, interminable and abominable, morbid and morbific, impious and impolite disputations about God, between Deist and Pantheist, and Atheist, Unitarian, Trinitarian, and Nothingarian—Monotheist and Polytheist, &c. &c., which find their rational solution in the Social Law, their sensuous solution in the harmonies of healthy and happy man with lovely and abounding nature, their sympathetic solution in the play of passional affinities in true society, and their integral or pivotal solution in the intuitional consciousness acting under these conditions.—E.

object of a regular study by analysis or synthesis, which would have disclosed to us, first the Social Destiny, afterwards the theory of the causes and ends of movement.

There can exist no unity between the three principles except as the active principle, or God, associates with the neuter or mathematical principle in moving or modifying the material or passive principle.

This alliance of the three principles constitutes fundamentally the unity of action, and to obtain unity of effect in his operations on movement, God must create *hieroglyphically*, whether in the passional or material sphere. He must ally His passions, ours, and those of the animals, as well as instincts and affinities, to the theorems of mathematics, and represent in every effect of movement, the general type, which are the passions of God united with the mathematics. To say that the passions of God and ours are the same, would be in appearance an insult to God. We should recall on this subject the duality of movement to which the passions are subject, the subversive and the harmonic as depicted in the roots of the tree and in its branches, to which add the analogy of the caterpillar and the butterfly, and in the sidereal movement of the comets and planets ; a duality which destroys nothing of unity since these two kinds of stars agree and gravitate combinedly on the same pivot. They are besides identical in essence since every planet has been a comet, and every comet will become a planet.

But the comets are in the phase of anterior transition, a phase in which the passions of our globe are also found during the course of the four dark limbos, the Savage, Patriarchal, Barbarous and Civilized estate, and although the passions in this transition still produce effects, like the seven permanent scourges,* diametrically opposite to their destiny, these are not less in unity with the general system of movement which admits at the two extremes of every career, countermovement, or subversion of properties and of results both physically and passionally.†

* These are :—

1\. Poverty. 2. Fraud. 3. Oppression. 4. Carnage.

5\. Derangement of seasons and deterioration of climates.

6\. Generation of pestilence, disease, and organic deterioration.

7\. Consolidation of ignorance in prejudice, and spiritual deterioration.

Y General Selfishness,
X Vicious Circle, } ⋈ Disunity of Man with God.
Ⅹ Duplicity of Action,

For these scourges which the passions perpetually reproduce during the incoherent periods organized in separate family households and individual competition in labor, Association by Passional Series substitutes seven permanent blessings and the Pivotal.

1\. General abundance. 2. Practical truth in all relations.

3\. Social guarantees and Providence. 4. Industrial armies.

5\. Progressive improvement in climates and Harmony of Seasons.

6\. Extinction of Contagions, and Unitary Hygiene.

7\. General enlightenment, encouragement of inventors, and institution of experiments in unexplored branches of movement.

Y Social Charity,
X Harmonic Progression, } ⋈ Unity of Man with God.
Ⅹ Unity of Action,

† This unity is admirably illustrated in the spiritual sphere by the effects of misfortune and suffering, which while they belong to

In virtue of this law our corporeal faculties, destined to secure to us the enjoyments of life, are in the ages of infancy and old age only pledges of suffering and of constraint. The child and the old man suffer infirmities, privations and constraint. Examine any

the subversive social periods and have generally by their accumulation an impoverishing and deteriorating influence on the soul, yet are also capable, as we observe, of forcing the soul in its reactions against them to take refuge with Christ in the bosom of God, and thus attain by an indirect impulse the same end of internal unity and of harmony, however truncated by external circumstances, which in the Harmonic Social periods we shall attain by direct impulse and in coincidence with material luxury and prosperity; when having found and conquered the kingdom of Heaven, in the order of the Passional Series, all these things—goods of the world and the senses shall be added unto us. In either case, the essential fact or aim of man's existence, Unity with God is attained; the important distinction lying here, that only the few, the exceptional category of souls, are susceptible of salvation by the reactive method or influence of misfortune, while all are susceptible of it through the influences of harmony. The churches are then justified by facts in their exclusive doctrines of election as regards the past and present of humanity, but this exclusiveness terminates and gives place to the fact of universal salvation from the epoch of the organization of the Passional Series. It was very well for Montaigne to say, "Misfortunes and afflictions shall never make me do anything except to curse them. I see clearest in fine weather."

Montaigne was a man of fortune, pleasantly situated in society, and possessing an exceptionally fine and well equilibriated organization. Being himself an anticipation in many respects of the man of harmonic periods, it is natural that he should have adopted the sentiments which there become practically true for the mass of mankind as they were for him. Yet the opposite doctrines of the discipline of suffering—"Whom God loveth he chasteneth," are more true for the civilized period in general. This interesting phenomenon of transition connecting the spiritual movement of the opposite social periods other branch of movement, you will always find the two extremes of a career in contradictory development to the whole in its collective aspect. A tree gives no fruit but much trouble in its two extreme ages, [still more an animal, and most of all man.] A fine genius

is thus described in a beautiful little book of analogies called "The Old Man's Home.

"And is it a pleasant path, Annie, that leads us home?"

"It is an up-hill path," she said; "but, as we walk along it, we can, if we will, awake soft notes of music beneath our feet, and there are whispering winds to cheer us on our way."

"And what, Annie," I asked, "do you mean by the soft music and the whispering wind?"

"The soft music is prayer," she replied, "and the whispering wind, the Holy Spirit of God."

"And can we," I said, "have the soft music without the whispering wind? I mean, can we pray without the assistance of God's Holy Spirit?" But there was no need for me to have explained the question; the language of allegory was most familiar to the mind of the child, and she had recourse to it in her reply. "No, sir," she said, "for the spirit of harmony dwells in the breeze; and it is the wind alone that gives life to the music, and bears it upward from earth to Heaven."

I cannot tell how far she realized the deep meaning of these words, for I did not venture to examine her upon them. I was afraid lest I should only render indistinct the image which they conveyed to her mind, by touching her colors with an unskilful hand.

Presently I resumed:—"It must, Annie, I think, be a pleasant path along which the winds thus murmur, and the music plays!"

"It is a pleasant path," she replied, "and yet it is very thickly covered with thorns." "But," she added, and from the smile which for a moment lit up her countenance, it seemed as though this were the metaphor which pleased her best, "they are all magic thorns; and if we look upward to the clear, blue sky, and tread firmly upon them, they change into flowers."

is also defective at the two extremes. A star is an incoherent comet before its implanation, then after having furnished the career of harmony, it is displaned, falls back into incoherence, and its residue, dissolved in the milky way, goes to furnish aliment to new stars.

The two transitions form general ties of movement

"And is there not another path," I said, venturing to guess at the conclusion of the allegory, "which leads away from home, and along which the flowers, as you tread upon them, keep changing into thorns?"

But I was wrong in my conjecture, for she looked perplexed, and replied, "I do not know, sir, about the other paths; the old man never used to talk to me but of one." And I felt ashamed of my question, as I said within myself, "Oh, happy child, to know as yet but of one path; and happy teacher, to have so shared the innocency of childhood as to have spoken to her but of one!"

Presently, however, she continued, as though she observed my confusion: "But, sir, he said there were flowers that grew by the wayside. When the winds blow softly upon them they perfume the air; and their fragrance is very sweet and pleasant to those who pass them by; but if we stop to gather them, then they become magic flowers, and keep changing into thorns. And do you know, sir, why it is so?"

"Not exactly," I replied; "I should like you to explain it to me."

"Because, sir," she said, "when we gather them, we stoop down, turn our eyes towards the earth, instead of gazing upward on the clear, blue sky."

"But, Annie," I observed, "you have not yet told me what are the flowers which we gather, or the thorns on which we tread."

"The thorns," she replied, "are the trials and afflictions which God sends us; the flowers are the pleasures and amusements which we make choice of for ourselves."

"Then, Annie," I said, "the children who gather the magic flowers are those who follow their own will [seeking pleasure before duty], while those who tread upon the magic thorns are such as submit themselves quietly to the will of God."

although their effects be subversive and contradictory with the general tone of the universe which offers $\frac{7}{8}$ths of harmony and $\frac{1}{8}$th of transitions. This contradiction does not prevent the transitions from connecting with the harmonic tone. Thus the Creator, in all the series of animals, plants, aromas and minerals, observes exactly the rule of transition or divergent and mixed species, like the eel, which forms the link of transitions between serpents and fishes; the flying-fish and the bat which connect fishes, quadrupeds and birds. The transition or duality to which movement is subject, so far from preventing its unity of system, is, on the contrary, its support; all created things (except the three principles) having a beginning and an end; their elements at these two epochs are in subversive development without having changed their nature but only their course.

Our passions being subject to this general law of movement, the odious effects which they present in the state of transition do not prevent them from being the twelve passions of God, and as a proof of it we shall soon admire in Harmony the results of the most fearful of all, which is Ambition. Every one seeing it in Harmony produce in every direction justice, truth and philanthropic virtues, will exclaim that Ambition is the noblest emanation of God. It will not however have changed its nature but only its course.*

* Zoroaster teaches that there is *one* first principle, infinite and eternal—Boundless Time. " In the greatness of time," he says, " there was no being who could call it creator, since none had yet been created. Then it created fire and water, and from their mixture, or when they

Once accustomed to speculate upon transition or duality, to consider it as a scaffolding necessary in our progress towards happy destinies, an inevitable obstruction, we shall no longer be astonished at the temporary reign of evil, and shall conceive that it exists by God's

had been created, proceeded Ormusd. Time was the creator, and preserved its empire over the creatures which it had produced."

This, translated from mystical into scientific phrase, means simply that all beings are subject to a law of organic periodicity, their appearance or birth depending on the preparation of the sphere or place and medium which they enter, and all the phenomena of their life being subject to a law of organic periodicity, which gives the varying characters of their formation or birth, growth, maturity, decline and death, disintegration or transformation.

Fire and water correspond to the oxygen and hydrogen principles—the oxygen principles are supporters of combustion, and of the transformation of tissues either living or dead, which is an act of slow combustion; the hydrogen principles are combustible, or bodies undergoing combustion and transformation. So in the vital organisms, to which hydrogen and water are always essential elements, we have the contrasted states and functions of activity and nutrition, of Doing and of Being, of Expression and Reception, which are terms equally true of our physical and of our spiritual life.

" In Boundless Time there is no distinction of good and evil, of just and unjust. In it all nature is stable or essential, and whatever forms its substance assumes in beings of the second or third order, it will always be the centre of perfection."

Illustrations.—If the erection of a building be considered as an act relative to the all-creative Time, we observe a natural division of two forms or directions of movement; first, in excavating the foundation, preparing the wood and stone materials, &c., we have an apparently confused and destructive process—holes dug—trees rooted up and sawn or cut to pieces, &c., a process strikingly contrasted with the subsequent operations of adjustment which present more and more as they advance the order and beauty of architectural symmetry and permission, because the reign of Good is sevenfold in duration, and there is no creation without admitting two transitions in the general system contradictory in their effect to the unitary whole.

adaptation to our uses and pleasures. Yet the analytic or destructive, equally with the synthetic part of this dual action, was necessary to the end attained; both equally essential and perfect in respect to the common time which encloses them. It is the same with a plant, whose dual movement consists, first, in sending forth roots or radicles incoherently downwards into the dark cold soil, there to absorb nutritive matter which prepares the subsequent rise of the leaves and branches converging in a unitary trunk, stem, or pivot, into the warm and sunlit air, where it becomes a centre of harmonic relations for many insects, larger animals, and perhaps for man. But in the *Boundless* all-enclosing *Time*, the first protrusion of the root is equally good and essential with the subsequent flowering or fruitage of the plant.

It is the same with an animal in respect to the dual and contrasted movement of its fœtal formation, where vital actions are seen to proceed at once from numerous points and centres not yet visibly related; and of its perfected organism, where at its appointed period all the parts are seen in their connection, and form a unitary life, self-controlling in regard to its internal relations, yet still, perhaps, incomplete in relation to the outward sphere in which it is destined to move, and to the race or planet, still in a fœtal state, of which it is only one minute element.

It is thus with an orchestra; we have a preparatory discord whilst the musicians are tuning their instruments, and a subsequent harmony in the accord of sweet sounds blending in a unitary theme—but the discord and the accord are equally essential and perfect in Boundless Time, where component parts are justified by their composed wholes.

Finally, it is thus in the social movement, in whose superior processes we ourselves are component elements, and where our passions are often too much involved to permit that consolation which we should derive from sympathy with the creative principle of Boundless

This stated, we shall easily see a unitary effect in the hideous furniture of our globe, in the thirty serpents, the forty-three stink-bugs, the tigers, the wolves, the rats, the sharks, the flies, the reptiles, and so many other demoniac works at whose creation the Deity certainly felt horror !

Time, permitted us by history and prophecy. If we would investigate the social movement with the same calm reason as we observe the *formation* of a *crystal* in a saturated *solution*, or the dual development in vegetable and animal organisms, or in any and every constructive fact of nature or art, wherever we have the completed process within our scope or view, we should not be dismayed that in an operation so extensive as the social order of a race, and the advent of harmony in a planet, the period of disorder and relative evil should be measured by centuries. This evil and disorder, so fraught with suffering to the present forms of our life, will be justified to us if the analogy of natural movement holds true, by other and happy forms and conditions of the same essential life, when those social periods, whose John the Baptist mission is the parallel development of industry, art, and science, and the propagation of the doctrines of Christunity, have completed their preparatory work in the organic structure of human society.

We may observe tnat the preparatory period of disorder is always short in comparison with the duration of the subsequent order in the examples cited, and any others. Thus from a period of social disorder, crime, and suffering of 5000 years, we are to infer a harmonic and happy period, brilliant with social virtues, of immense duration, in which our race will soon outgrow the scrofula of a sickly infancy and the pains attendant on the development of its industrial faculties, which are the teeth with which it is to chew nature. The printing press. the steam engine, the electro-magnetic apparatus, and gun-cotton are some of these teeth.

Each evil and suffering experienced by man, becomes in the course of Time the parent cause of its opposite good. So to the pangs of hunger we owe the knowledge and art of obtaining and preparing our

But these unclean creatures were essential to hieroglyphical Unity. In fact, the four cardinal movements being calculated upon the passional, a globe which is passing through the transition or ascending subversion, must receive for this phase of movement an apparatus analogous to the effects of the human passions, to which all is coordinate; and if we examine the immense and abominable treacheries which our passions engender in the civilized, barbarous and savage limbos, we shall conclude that God must, for unity, have modelled their effects in the infernal furniture adapted to the ascending transition, and from which we may be delivered within five years by a new creation, which will follow immediately on the foundation of Harmony, and will furnish land and sea with legions as precious and charming as the present are odious. Will it be thought that to compensate us for the misfortune of entering into a phase of subversion, or ascending transition, God should

food: to those of cold, our beautiful cloth fabrics and comfortable dwellings, &c., not only valuable to us in themselves, but from the development of our faculties in their attainment. Thus likewise of our spiritual and social evils, which knot man's heartstrings into a lash, and scourge him unremittingly through the career of his incoherent societies, towards the goal of harmony. Give him a little comfort, safety from imminent destruction, a few luxuries, and he stagnates in a paltry individualism; it is only by keeping his aspirations beyond all proportion to his attainments, and by overwhelming him with perils and sufferings, that God has fairly cornered man, and driven him to discover and seek to realize his social destiny, in whose combinations and distributions, individual passions and tastes, whether material or spiritual, find for the first time their healthy development and satisfaction.—E.

give us a good creation, an abundance of useful animals and plants? He could not do so without violating the law of hieroglyphic unity, for if he gave good creations to the globes which are about to pass through their periods of misfortune, he would admit in principle the contrast of creation with the effects of passions, thence it would be necessary to adapt infernal furniture like ours to ages of harmony, whose duration is sevenfold that of the subversive periods. There would be duplicity and absurdity in such an order. Many ideas plausible on their first aspect are really monstrosities. Such is the moral precept to prefer virtue to riches and despise riches, which can only be obtained at the expense of virtue. It is necessary then, according to this rule, to despise attraction, and consequently to despise God who is the author of attraction, and who has given to it a hundred times more influence than to virtuous maxims. Now to conciliate in this precept the respect due to God and to virtue, let us say that we must, through obedience to God, love riches, since they form the first of the three attractive impulses to which He subjects us :—

Three passional foci,	Correspond-ing to
1. Luxury, ...	Material Incarnation.
2. Social Groups, ...	Divine Love.
3. Serial Order, ...	Mathematical Wisdom.

At the same time, in order to walk in the ways of God, we must seek an order of things in which love of riches may be compatible with the practice of virtue.

Such is the property of the state of Harmony or mechanism of the passional Series. [The inadequacy of individual or private virtue is shown in the fact that examples of stoical or even *Christian* virtue, which is something better, although the best things we have yet, have never been able to determine general imitation by their attractiveness, that the characters most unexceptionable and amiable in their personal relations, are seldom the chosen instruments of great social or industrial progress, and that nature often shows her contempt for all our moral distinctions by overwhelming the virtuous with evils and misfortunes, and even producing evil (during the subversive periods) from their attempts at good, as sometimes good from the reckless energies of those whom morality condemns.

The slave trade, with all its climax of horrors, has already produced extensive and incontestible good, especially to the negro, and will ultimately justify its past by immense uses of the highest order to both races, while the missionary enterprise in the South Seas, undoubtedly commenced and sustained with the best intention, has proved one of the most deplorably pernicious facts in the history of man. It has presided over the destruction of one of his finest races. See first edition of *Melville's Omoo.* The terrors of the church have suppressed it in the last. See also a series of papers published in the *New York Weekly Universe*, for 1850.

So vain is it for man to contend against the order of Nature, which decrees $\frac{7}{8}$ths of evil for the whole period of the incoherent movement, and reserves social virtues and harmonies as well as beautiful and friendly creations of plants and animals for Societies which absorb Selfishness by the order of Passional Series.—E.]

It is clear that wisdom in the theory of attraction is very different from the wisdom of morality, and it is truly on this subject that it is necessary, according to Bacon, to reform the human understanding and to forget all that we have learned.

Some gleams of virtue appear in civilization, *rari nantes in gurgite vasto.* God has represented them in a small number of societary and honorable animals, as the elephant, the dog, the horse, and other beneficent species which form an infinitely small minority in the crowd of evil-doers. The good animals figure in their present connection only under title of transitions and links with the system of the next creation, $\frac{7}{8}$ths of whose products will be associated with man. Consequent upon the general law of transition we shall see in these harmonic creations about $\frac{1}{8}$th of evil products or subversive creatures, if not hostile to man, at least useless for his service and hurtful to his servants or domestic animals and garden plants. This $\frac{1}{8}$th of evil will be necessary in a beneficent creation, because movement requiring connection in its branches, the creations or apparatus adapted to ages of harmony must be linked by $\frac{1}{8}$th to that of subversive ages, as we see the present furniture of our planet connected by $\frac{1}{8}$th of good products with the system of the next creations. Conformably to the law of transitions, the present furniture should depict some effects of future harmony yet unattained by us. For example, in the animal kingdom the Bee and the Beaver; in the vegetable, the Pansy and the Cacao are hieroglyphics of some social effects of Harmony, but to explain their analogies the reader must be familiar with the mechanism of the Passional Series. A few Sketches may however solace the impatient.

The Beaver represents domestic unity or the combined home. The Beavers do not, like our villagers, construct as many houses as couples; they build a collective habitation, as will be the manor house of a phalanx of fifteen hundred persons, where there will be lodgings of every degree of cost, but a single house of the size of a small town, with communications or sheltered internal galleries, warmed in winter and ventilated in summer; then sanded and ornamented subterranean passages from the dwelling to the stables and stores. All these precautions are necessary to excite industrial attraction, to favor activity and the intrigues of Series without interruption by changes of weather.

The Beaver does not represent all the details in his house, but he shows us the general principle of *combination.* Thus is the building both aquatic and terrestrial, combining even the elements. This property alone suffices to give the allegorical key note, most hieroglyphics being created in an abridged style. It is thus of the Bee and the Wasp. The Bee offers a spectacle which has always puzzled thinkers. They have said of this insect what they ought to have thought of all nature. Every one has opined that the hive was a beautiful enigma that Providence gives us to guess, but all creatures, from the Elephant to the Flea, have this same property. They are so many pretty quizzes that come saying, "What is my thought like?"

None is more worthy our attention than the beehive. The philosophers have found in it an emblem of their favorite chimera, equality and fraternity; yet the bees kill the drones when their service is finished. Now it is hardly a very fraternal procedure to knock people on the head when we have no longer need of them. The hive does not represent fraternity and still less equality, for the working bees respectfully serve the queen, who is by her conformation, her rank and her functions, their superior.

What is then the sense of this enigma? Behold it: The hive represents the unitary government of the globe in harmony, all free commerce being a crime against the state, which would spoliate at once the producer and the administration. It is the part which free commerce actually plays, it spoliates sovereigns and subjects under pretext of supplying their wants.

The commercial relations of Harmony are far more extensive than ours. They may be estimated at twenty fold, for every phalanx or canton is assorted in provisions from all parts of the globe. If in so extended a social mechanism it were necessary to be subjected to those legions of cheats called merchants, brokers, usurers, stock-jobbers, monopolists, &c., to experience frauds, to operate with uncertainty and distrust, relations would be everywhere paralyzed, as they would now be in the currency if every merchant were allowed to throw into circulation moneys of his own making and of doubtful value.

All these chances of fraud are prevented in Harmony by the subjugation of the intermediary function, commerce. Circulation is made free all over the globe, but commerce is a clerk subordinated to the two functions of administration and production.

In emblem of this subordination, the working Bee (productive function) kills the drone when it no longer needs him. As to the two classes, productive and administrative (worker and queen), they are united, not by subordination, but by sincere and devoted affection. Thus the whole swarm deserts the hive if the queen happens to leave it. It is the emblem of that passional union which in harmony reigns between the people and their chiefs. These, in the Societary order, are of thirteen progressive classes, from the chiefs of a township to those of the entire globe which form the thirteenth degree or diapason. The hive does not represent these smaller details, it is limited to depict the simple function of a chief or queen in active service, with all the towns represented by the alveoli, and in passional accord with their inhabitants, represented by the working bees, each of which represents, not an individual, but a Phalanx. Individuals are not equal in Harmony, but towns enjoy a political equality, having all the same right to the protection of the Unitary government.

The wasp nest, hieroglyphic of the civilized movement, produces nothing, despite its immense labor, whence the only result is a grey paper. The hive, on the contrary, gives a double or compound product by honey and by wax. There are beautiful allegorics on the employment of these two products, symbols of the luxury and of the unity which reign in Harmony. Let us only remark that what produces nothing to man is a hieroglyphic of evil, *i.e.*, of the civilized, barbarous, patriarchal and savage estates.

Man being pivot of the creation, every being that does not combine with him by services or affections, or charms of some kind in a simple or a compound manner, is necessarily a hieroglyphic of the limbic societies. Witness those ignoble laborers, the ant, the spider and the wasp, who soil our dwellings or pillage our provisions, whilst the hieroglyphics of combined labor, the bee and the beaver, give a double product, one by its wax and honey, the other by a magnificent fur and an antidote, the castoreum ; [not to mention its flesh, of which the tail, trowel or organ of labor is esteemed delicious.]

System makers and unveilers of the mysteries have not thought of this distinction between productive and unproductive labor to explain the created emblems. Thus they boast the *Toad* and the *Spider ;* it is as if they boasted baseness and lying. Let us finish our analysis, we have still to examine the Heartsease and the Cacao tree.

THE PANSY OR HEARTSEASE.

The *Pansy* produces nothing: then it is the hieroglyphic of some vicious effect of passion. Thus a civilizee will reason, seeing no real product but in current money. Gross error, the flower of the Heartsease, far from being unproductive, gives a composite or double product, combining charm with instruction. Let us explain the enigma.

This flowret is an enigma of harmony: to conceive its meaning we must know that every phalanx or population of a town is divided as to ages into sixteen choirs freely classed, for all is free in harmony. But from motives unknown in civilization, every one finds his advantage in ranking himself with the choir to which his age nearly corresponds. Among the sixteen amphichoirs or thirty-two choirs, there are only twenty-four of active harmony, of which:

2. Cherubim,	male and female,	ages	4	to	6
3. Seraphim,	"	"	6	"	8½
4. Lyceans,	"	"	8½	"	11½
5. Gymnasians,	"	"	11½	"	15
6. Youth,	'	"	15	"	19
The 1st, Infants and small children out of active harmony,	. . . . .		0	"	4

The functions and relations of the five choirs of children are represented in the five petals of the Pansy; three petals colored yellow and violet surmount the two all violet petals. Now the yellow, being color of parentage, is an indication that the three choirs, 4, 5, 6, ought to serve as parents to the choirs 2d and 3d, whose two hieroglyphic petals are placed below the three others, and this hierarchy in ages and functions is the pledge of unity, depicted by the white (color of unity), which borders the petals.

These three tribes, 4th, 5th and 6th, are themselves subordinated in the mechanism of ascending corporate charm, which is the mainspring of harmonic education, to the seven choirs of high harmony, in sign of which nature has placed seven rays which touch upon the yellow. The attraction of children is in perfect accord with this hierarchy, for the child hates to be lectured by parents and schooled by pedants ; he is spontaneously regardful and imitative of other children a little more advanced in age and force. Hence the two choirs, 2 and 3, are pleased to recognize the supremacy of the choirs 4, 5 and 6. The lesson of subordination which the Heartsease gives them is only the expression of their preference. It orders only what pleases them. The lesson is not less precious in teaching children that God himself has regulated their duties, and that all his decisions are recorded in the productions of nature, and that we should give them no precept without supporting it on the decrees of God, permanently represented in all nature, and conformable to attraction, to the child's inclination. Arguing from this conformity, we excite in children the love and admiration of that Creator who only commands them pleasure, and who impresses on their characters natural inclinations for all the duties which he expects of them.*

Let us examine some problem of Universal Unity by the help of the Pansy. It makes part of the universe, as does every plant, animal or mineral, and if we admit that man also is a part of the universe, there must be unitary relations between the passional man or the distribution of passions made to man, and the distribution of properties made to a plant such as the Pansy.

1st. *Problem of Material Movement.*—If a man placed at a window, and holding in his hand a bouquet of the Pansy, let it fall into the street, what laws of gravitation will the bouquet follow in its fall? A fine question truly; it will fall according to the laws common to all bodies, acceleration in an unequal progression determined by Galileo. If we are all agreed on this point, we then admit that the flower called Heartsease is unitary with the universe in a material sense in the impulsion of material movement. In this case why should it not be unitary with the universe in what re-

* The organization of the Passional Series or Social Mathematics for which characters with their instincts and passions have been calculated, being always premised. Out of this order pleasure is treacherous and evasive, and attraction presents only an extricable enigma; individual action being equally false in ascetics who compress their passions, in libertines who abuse them, and in the moderates who temporize and coquet with pleasure and duty, principle and expediency, without being true to any. All under one form or another carry their cross, and the world presents one wide scene of passional crucifixion, until the spirit of Christ's life and teaching shall find a home in the Social frame of the Combined order or Passional Series.—E.

gards the four movements, Aromal, Organic, Instinctual and Passional? If you admit that there is unity of man with the universe, of which this flower is a part, it must be recognized as unitary and concordant with the laws of the passional movement as with those of the four other movements.

2d. *Problem of Aromal Movement.*—Why is the Pansy deprived of perfume, although it is a species of the Violet, which is strongly perfumed? What were the motives of God in this refusal of the generic aroma of the Violet? What are the analogies of this disposition with the properties of the human passions and with the theorems of mathematics; invariable rule in the operations of God?

3d. *Problem of the Organic Movement.*—Why has God chosen that three of the petals should surmount the two others, and should be half of yellow and violet, while the two lower are limited to the violet shade? Why have all the five the property of a white bordering? And why is the leaf of the Pansy scolloped in graduated points in ascending and descending series, in contradistinction to the leaf of the Violet, which is round? Finally, why does one hide under its leaves, above which the other majestically rises? What is the analysis of all these dispositions with the properties of the human passions?

5th. *Problem of the Passional Movement.*—What are the functions of social mechanics represented by this flower?

⋈ *Problem of Unity.*—What is the relation of the

five petals of the Pansy with the five planets, Mercury, Juno, Ceres, Pallas and Vesta? What modifications of these stars and their influences are connected with the endowment of perfume to this flower, and what changes in the planet we inhabit?

Great matter of astonishment in all these questions! Yet their solution ought not to embarrass one who knows the laws of the unity of the universe, and if our fine wits beat a retreat on such problems, it is a virtual avowal that their prate about the unity of the universe is mere charlatanism. They know none of its laws except those of the material movement, and they do not yet know how to apply these to the passions of man.

There are some for which plain good sense suffices. Witness the relation of the passions with the Galilean progression, the acceleration of fall, or simple tendency towards the centre of attraction. It exists in the tendency to fortune, and a merchant who shall have gained one thousand dollars the first year will find it still easier to gain three thousand the second year, and so on in this order:

1st	year,	$1,000	1st	second,	1 yard.
2d	"	3,000	2d	"	3 "
3d	"	5,000	3d	"	5 "
4th	"	7,000	4th	"	7 "
5th	"	9,000	5th	"	9 "

Thus fortune is an avalanche which swells as it moves, and is only difficult to seize in its germ. We should not as easily discover the relations of other laws of movement with fortune and with the passions, because certain laws representing effects of harmony become incomprehensible to us, while this which represents civilization becomes sensible to us. Thus our passions in certain effects of the actual order are unitary with some laws of the material movement, but to know their general unity with all the laws we must know the effects of the passions in harmony. Even in material movement the only branch whose laws are known to us, we cannot make their unitary application or deduce thence the unity of man with the universe. Our ignorance is much worse in the other branches.*

2d Problem.—Why is the Pansy deprived of per fume, etc.? Because it indicates the effects of ambition among the infantile choirs. The flowers hieroglyphic of ambition, are deprived of perfume, the Tulip, Ranunculus, Anemone, &c. The Violet, another variety of the same species as the Pansy, has much perfume, but it is hieroglyphic of friendship, a group whose dominant tone is gaiety, in case of an assemblage of seven persons as an average term in the combination

* Other unities of the passions with the law of gravitation are exposed in my work on *Homœopathy*, page 36, and consecutive. The contrasted effects of presence and absence from their natural objects correspond with those of distance in gravitation. In the one case the effect is measured by the time or duration of absence, in the other by the number of miles, and by increasing either to a certain extent the attraction of passion or of gravity becomes so feeble as to be practically null; though I shall not undertake to define how many months or years of a lover's absence may be equal to a removal beyond the sphere of erotic gravitation towards his or her pivotal star.—E.

of groups ; and as the group of ambition even in Harmony gives the tone of gravity to all relations, God, for the fidelity of the portrait, has denied perfume even in the flowers of a family highly aromatized, as to the Pansy, a sort of Violet. This rule is not without exception. The flowers of ambition take the hypermajor perfume when they are like the Lily, of compound creation, or due to the intervention of two planets with the Sun.

The rest of them preserve a small dose of aroma quite analogous to their passional hieroglyphic; witness the Tulip, hieroglyphic of individual justice, and the Ranunculus, hieroglyphic of assemblies of civilized etiquette. The Tulip bears in the interior of its calyx a slight bitter perfume, in symbol of actual justice, a true cup of bitterness for every civilizee who will practice it. The Ranunculus, isolated, has no sensible odor, but a bunch of these flowers slightly agitated exhale a delicate herbaceous perfume, which amateurs duly appreciate. Thus etiquette without stiffness does not fail to charm in a numerous and brilliant assembly, but it is very insipid in *tête-à-tête ;* and by analogy, the Ranunculus yields a sensible perfume only when grouped in numbers, forming a column of aromas united. As this etiquette proscribes the free development of love, God, by analogy, has refused to the Ranunculus the azure blue color, which is that of Love. If he has also refused it to theTulip, it is because there is no more justice when love enters into contest with civilized justice. Hence the flower hieroglyphic of justice must not dress in blue. It is also refused to other flowers very richly draped, as the Carnation and the Anemone. It would take too long to explain why.

Different flowers, among others the Iris with three corollas, are subject to change their perfume without changing their species. The problem becomes more interesting than that of the Violet, which changes the species in omitting the aroma of the Pansy, whilst the Iris loses it in changing only the variety. Let us seek the cause of this in the passion represented. The Iris is the hieroglyphic of marriage, now there are many varieties of marriage : there are very happy and very unhappy marriages. Some charming families are depicted by the perfumed blue, yellow and butterfly Iris ; others, insipid and disagreeable, by the wall Iris, whose aspect is rather savage, and whose crushed leaf ending in a dry withered point, alludes to the vexatious details of poor families. The mixed grey Iris, very tall and majestic, but dull and without perfume, depicts the marriage of speculative ambition without love or charm, as those of kings. The butterfly Iris, rich in perfume and graceful in its color, depicts the marriages of lovers : [pictures furnished by colors and forms are types of organic movement]. The large pale azure and yellow Iris, whose bearing and perfume are very agreeable, depict good marriages in the easy circumstances of the moneyed classes, where the links of parentage engender a semblance of love between parties in whose union Love was not the ruling power. Thus this Iris takes only a pale azure color of half love, while it displays in strong and beautiful shades the yellow color of parentage, and of the prosperous marriages where ease and the peace of the household reign. The blue Raymond Iris, half indigo, depicts good marriages without children, less strong in the domestic tie; those whose union is limited to a cabalistic concert without family affections. Their mainspring of charm is a tie of Love and of habit, with a strong dose of cabalism. Thus their hieroglyphic flower is of a mixed shade, between azure and indigo, with a remainder of perfume, much less than in the pale azure and yellow Iris. This perfume which declines in the blue Raymond, becomes quite extinct in the dull or slate-blue of the wall Iris, emblem of peasant marriages and of the sweet pleasures enjoyed under the thatch.

Nature seems to consider them rather insipid, since she withdraws all perfume from the symbolic flower, whose aspect is sad and poor like the conjugal unions of the peasantry. It quite abandons the blue to take a deeper shade of indigo, color of cabalism. Thus the class depicted think only of the "*tin*," and carry into their household a calculating, scheming spirit instead of Love [whose natal sphere is luxury and beauty in all externals, and which, in their long privation, takes flight to escape the wear and tear and vulgar companionship of base necessities]. A few exceptions only confirm the general rule.

These few details on the distribution of aromas enable us to conceive how the aromal movement is one with the passional, that it is coordinated hieroglyphically to the properties of the passions, to those of Harmony in the flower of the Pansy, to those of civilization in the Iris and Ranunculus. We shall rise from these subaltern analogies to those which embrace the aromal system of the universe. Every perfume being distributed by a planet, the flower depicting some effect of love as the Iris, ought to be a product of the planets which have this passion dominant. Hence the Iris, which represents Marriage, a contract, of real or similated love, is a creation of Herschel, cardinal of Love, who rules the eight notes or hyperminor satellites composing the gamut of Love in aromal mechanics.

As to the Tulip and Ranunculus, which paint effects of ambition, we owe the first to Saturn, cardinal of Ambition, and the second to Proteus, an ambigu annexed to his scale. The Pansy, although hieroglyphic of ambition, is only so on one side, it springs from a type of Friendship, the Violet; both are of the earth's own aromas and not of Saturn's.

By initiating ourselves into the general system of creations, we shall determine the laws of unity between the passional man and the entire universe, from the functions of planetary systems to the properties of the least creatures as the Jessamine, Violet and Pansy, where we shall everywhere find faithful pictures of our passions and the universal unity of the system of God on the five movements, of which the four cardinal are subordinated to the passional or pivotal.

3d. *Problem of the Organic Movement.*—Why has God chosen that three petals of the Pansy should surmount, etc., see page 226. The two amphi-choirs of cherubim and seraphim, Nos. 2 and 3, are judged in their little debates by the amphi-choirs of the Lyceans, Gymnasians and Youth, Nos. 4, 5 and 6. It will be seen in the Treatise on Education (*Universal Unity*, vol. iv), that a contest among children is not judged by their fathers but by their peers : it is carried according to its nature either before the senate of the Little Bands, [supreme police of the flower garden and orchard], or before the divan of the Little Hordes, [supreme police of the domestic animals], or before the Vestalic Synod [which rules in the sphere of social etiquette] ; three chambers drawn from the three amphi-choirs 4, 5, and 6. This subordination is indicated by the position of the two violet petals beneath the three half of yellow, the parental color. All five take the white bordering, color of unity, in sign of the concurrence of the five amphi-choirs in the productive mechanism of active Harmony. The five streaks in the centre of the yellow, whose rays are directed to the centre, indicate the same coincidence.

The violet, typical flower of the class to which the Pansy belongs, is reduced to a single color, although its five petals are the same in form. This is because the Violet represents only the germ of the 1st choir, the Bambins, whence the five others are to issue. Thus its leaf is confusedly rounded, while that of the Pansy is scolloped out in tongues as a serial picture of the five series of amphi-choirs. The Violet alone has the perfume, because its infantile choir of Bambins, is yet exempt from ambitious intrigues. It is all for industry and relations of friendship, wherefore its flower bears only the aroma of simple friendship. It hides itself under the leaves in sign of the humble part which the bambins play in a Phalanx, where, until the age of five, they are excluded from the honors of active Harmony, unless they can anticipate their age and sooner pass the trials of admission into the choir of cherubim.

Let us add some picture drawn from another flower already cited, the Iris. Why is it formed of three calices assembled on one centre? Why these three flowers in one? It is because marriage is a compound of three groups thus connected in one:

1st. Familism: chief aim of marriage in regard to the species.

2d. Love: (at least material) which is the agent, and sometimes the germ, at others the result.

3d. Ambition: which is still another of the elements of marriage, for it is a league of industry and of fortune between the parties conjoined.

God has very distinctly represented in the trinary cup of the Iris these three elementary passions of marriage. There is no contract so notoriously founded in constraint. Thus one of the species is subjected to the other, and the superior, which is man, would hardly be less the slave of his partner if he fulfilled the duties imposed on him, both being equally excluded either from love or from the recognition of children born out of marriage. Nature has depicted this state of erotic servitude by crushing the plant, which develops itself all flattened, as though it were compressed between two boards which left for its growth only a narrow cleft of a line in breadth.

The Iris, as a picture of the conjugal couple, bears on every stalk two corollas [emblems of pleasure], and not more, one of which is above the other; but the second or inferior develops itself only when the first is withered. This is symbolic of the conjugal hierarchy, wherein the second, inferior and younger party, the woman, has no passional expansion but in the absence of the husband, whether by his death, which leaves a free field for the widow, or by the enchantment of her arts which nullify masculine authority, so that woman's liberty begins where the power of man ends. Wherefore the second corolla of the Iris almost invisible in bud, rises and expands only after the withering of the first. They cannot flourish simultaneously and expand together, since liberty in marriage cannot be the special attribute of both spouses. Exceptions may be cited, but nature paints every passional effect in general thesis, and not in the exception [whose conditions when analyzed only confirm the rule]. We must also observe that she always depicts the caste in which a passional effect is most prominent. If an effect of coarseness, it will be the populace rather than the great. If of etiquette, she will choose the most elevated class. Thus the Ranunculus faithfully depicts the king amid his court. He is represented in the ruffled scarlet Ranunculus. See page 141.

4th. *Problem of Instinctual Movement.*—What are the animals whose instincts and properties are hieroglyphically represented in the flower of the Pansy? It is very difficult to satisfy curiosity on this point. The two creations which form the lymbic furniture of our globe would give us 540 quadrupeds, to wit:

The Compound Subversive Ascendant on the old Continent, ...	405	540
The Simple Subversive Ascendant on the new Continent, ...	135	

Only 370 are found, and we may at most reckon 400, comprising the few which may yet be discovered in unexplored countries.

There remains then a vacuum of 140 species absent by abortion or destruction in germ, which analogy required in our subversive creations in order to paint faithfully the social facts of abortion and premature infantile deaths in the very outset of their mundane career, to which so many children are liable during the absence of sanatory providence and violation of physiological harmonies in the societies of incoherence. It is then the species depicting infancy and its social characters on which the heaviest loss might be expected to fall in abortive creations, and among these are, the five quadrupeds of Harmony (*diëzës*, and the five of Harmony *bémolisés)*, neuter, which are represented in the Pansy flower. They would be miniature creatures, adapted to the labors of infancy, as the dwarf horse, dwarf ox, dwarf camel, buffalo and onagra, whose intervention in labor would have been of eminent utility and of inestimable price, not by the little work they could have done, but by the societary combinations they would have excited among the assemblies of children which are so easy in small towns. The child is nearer to nature than the civilized man, more apt to listen to her suggestions.

There is little doubt that if children had had their dwarf quadrupeds, and had organized for their collective amusement various trivial works that every town would have permitted them, they would soon have invented some parts of the mechanism of the Passional Series; the fathers struck with their economy would have applied them to labors on a large scale, and it would have been a powerful advance towards the discovery of the complete mechanism.

[Every one knows the enthusiasm of children for dogs, Shetland ponies, &c., the imitative mania which makes it necessary for them to cooperate in any movement they see in progress, and their inclination for corporate or collective action. Put these passional facts together and Fourier's conclusion is inevitable. I shall give at the end of the work a note on the mechanism of the Passional Series. In the year 1814, the boys of Geneva actually organized spontaneously an army of 5000, which was as well disciplined and perfect in its maneuvres as any in Europe. Bernard, their General, was aged twelve.—E.]

5th. *Problem of the Passional Movement.*—What are the functions of the social mechanism represented by the Pansy flower? I cannot indicate the details of this analogy until I have given in the theory of asociation (*Unité Universelle*, Tome iv) a picture of the series of passional functions of the third power, of thirty-two notes or genera and the pivotal. We shall there recognize very distinctly the ten functions of children, of whom the Pansy flower is hieroglyphic in its five petals, emblems of the five active choirs below or at the commencement of puberty.

⋈ *Problem of Unity* (see page 226).—The answer, like that of the last problem, is deferred. These are questions which can only be resolved in a general treatise, and whose indication would not be appreciable to readers not initiated into the planetary destiny and aromal mechanism of the stars. We shall not then be astonished that I limit myself to state the problem, with ability of solving it to the entire satisfaction of the curious.

The previous solutions will suffice, I think, to establish that the theory of passional harmony obtained by the analytic and synthetic calculation of attraction, is the only science which can realize the aims of genius and initiate us into the mysteries of Universal Unity. [Whether the solutions presented be correct or not is trivial, this is all the algebra of science, in which we often make use of hypothecated values—xs and ys, which illustrate just as well as definite figures, the formula of operation. It is Fourier's fashion to dogmatize. Those who call themselves professors of the exact sciences will only laugh at these solutions where with great parade of system and precision of method they have only a scientific drama or amusement, since the questions at issue are light and fanciful, and the data are frequently postulates. I have only to repeat to them the old proverb, "He laughs best who laughs last."—E.]

It is clear that to explain the general links of movement which some of the wise have suspected, we must embrace the whole of the five branches of movement, and coordinate the four cardinal branches to the passional or pivotal, which is calculated on the mathematics. This distribution is the only one which embraces nature entire, as I shall show by the five questions stated on the flower of the Pansy, and its connections with entire nature in five branches, following the clue of the passional calculus or social destiny of the passions.

In this work I limit myself to the amusing side of the question. Its useful side is the theory of association, the art of suddenly attaining great riches and social concord, without which we can do nothing with great knowledge. It would be for *us* only an additional burden, a new disgrace! For what is more shameful for reason and genius than successes which satisfy none of the demands which man makes of them.

Is it not an insult to his misery to offer him every day torrents of light when he asks only one science, which shall universalize wealth?

[Those who have read the section on the Little Hordes in the "*New Industrial World*," will be pleased to meet here the analogy of the Cacao, as given by Fourier, though the honors of this tree have been contested in favor of the Date Palm. See page 88.]

THE CACAO represents the corporations of the Little Hordes, or the sufferings of industrial friendship. Its trunk is disposed oppositely to that of the Grape, which represents the enjoyments of friendship. The Cacao despoils itself of its numerous flowers, in allusion to the Little Hordes, who are the corporation most devoted to fatigues and the most disdainful of pleasures. Thus the tree seems designedly to reject the flower, emblem of pleasure ; it delights in the places which the Little Hordes frequent, in the wet soils, which they dry up, and in those which undergo violent commotions, as by a clearing or a fire. These habits are analogous to those of the Little Hordes, who prefer the most painful labors. Its fruit is the most oleaginous, (oil is the emblem of light and luxury) ; thus the corporation of the Little Hordes is that which furnishes most to luxury, inasmuch as it is a pivot of industrial attraction. Its oil, employed to anoint the limbs for wrestling or for pains, is exempt from all odor. Cleanness must be the attribute of the juice of a fruit representing the corporation of cleanliness, the Little Hordes, who [by homœopathic application of the passion of boys for dirt] deliver the manor of the combined order from filth, and drain its muddy grounds, and exterminate nuisances of all sorts.

Its fruit is very bitter, by analogy with the sufferings of the Little Hordes, but as they are the body most essential to the support of the unity, it combines well with sugar, emblem of Unity, and with the aromas of Unity—*vanilla canella*, &c.

The tree forms itself in a crown in allusion to the circle, which is the curve of Unitary Friendship, dominant passion of the Little Hordes. As this is the earliest at work of all the corporations of Harmony, it was proper that the hieroglyphical fruit should furnish the morning nourishment of man, and there is none more wholesome or more delicious than chocolate in its fluid form. Many Civilizees do not digest it, because they are not accustomed to it from childhood, and because they have generally weak stomachs; but when digested, there is nothing better after rising, as a tonic to the stomach and preparer of the appetite. Thus in Harmony it will be almost in universal use at three and four o'clock in the morning, before the early breakfast at five, to which the Hordes will come with a devouring appetite produced by exercise and chocolate. The Cacao is by the aroma of the moon Pallas or Esculapius, which perfumes with bitter and gives medicines.

[The common article sold as chocolate is a vile and adulterated profanity. The genuine chocolate, as found in Caraccas and Nicaragua, and prepared in cake, either pure or with sugar and vanilla, after boiling it a few moments in milk until properly dissolved, is at once food and drink, and the most integral and sustaining nourishment. It appears from the history of the American Indians enslaved to labor by the Spaniards, that they endured everything while their favorite Cacao was left them, but sank and died under their burdens when this was refused them by the officious cruelty of a royal and ecclesiastical decree. It was an inverse refinement in passional hygiene, worthy the spirit of the Inquisition.

Chocolate is no less adapted to sustain prolonged and ardent intellectual labor. Less intense in its stimulant quality than Coffee, it has not its febrile and nerve disturbing action, but is a true food of the nerves, which would make a great improvement in the general health of our people if substituted for coffee and tea as a general beverage. It must be made for this purpose pure, and rich and thick, for nothing is more contemptible than the greasy, dirty warm water that is usually called Cocoa or Chocolate. Fourier speaks of the Cacao as an *inverse* pivot, in its scale. This corresponds to the functions of the Hordes, who though a most honorable corporation in active harmony, are yet moved not by direct passional attraction in their heroic sacrifices and unpaid works in behalf of Unity. It is the point of honor, duty and devotion, without regard to direct attraction, which actuates them in offering $\frac{1}{8}$th of their fortune in unitary charity, and in forestalling all discontent by choosing for their share the most repulsive labors, and those which if performed for lucre rather than honor and charity, might degrade the class identified with them. Every truly pious and heroic soul will love Fourier at once on reading his chapter on the Little Hordes. We are to discriminate well between the harmonic *inversions* of movement in the Passional Series, characterized by the supremacy of the *spiritual* over the *material* element, as in the Little Hordes, the Vestalate and the Faquirate, and those passional inversions which belong to the incoherent movement, and which are characterized by the absorption of social and unitary tendencies in a base selfishness.—E.]

THE STAR AND THE LILY.

An old chieftain sat in his wigwam quietly smoking his favorite pipe, when a crowd of Indian boys and girls suddenly entered, and with numerous offerings of tobacco, begged him to tell them a story. Then the old man began :—

" There was once a time when this world was filled with happy people, when all nations were as one, and the crimson tide of war had not began to roll. Plenty of game was in the forest and on the plains. None were in want, for a full supply was at hand. Sickness was unknown. The beasts of the field were tame, they came and went at the bidding of man. One unending spring gave no place for winter—for its cold blasts or its unhealthy chills. Every tree and bush yielded fruit

Flowers carpeted the earth ; the air was laden with their fragrance, and redolent with the songs of married warblers, that flew from branch to branch, fearing none, for there were none to harm them. There were birds then of more beautiful song and plumage than now.

It was at such a time, when earth was a paradise and

man worthily its possessor, that the Indians were the lone inhabitants of the American wilderness. They numbered millions, and living as Nature designed them to live, enjoyed its many blessings. Instead of amusements in close rooms, the sports of the field were theirs. At night they met on the wide green fields. They watched the stars; they loved to gaze at them, for they believed them to be the residences of the good who had been taken by the Great Spirit.

One night they saw one star that shone brighter than the others. Its location was far away in the South near a mountain peak. For many nights it was seen, at length it was doubted by many that the star was as far distant in the Southern skies as it seemed to be. This doubt led to an examination, which proved the star to be only a short distance, and near the tops of some trees.

A number of warriors were deputed to go and see what it was. They went, and on their return said it appeared strange and somewhat like a bird. A committee of the wise men were called to inquire into, and if possible ascertain the meaning of the strange phenomena.

They feared that it might be the omen of some disaster. Some thought it a precursor of good, others of evil, and some supposed it to be the star spoken of by their forefathers as the forerunner of a dreadful war.

One moon had nearly gone by, and yet the mystery remained unsolved.

One night a young warrior had a dream, in which a

beautiful maiden came and stood at his side, and thus addressed him :—

"Young brave! charmed with the life of thy fore-fathers, its flowers, its birds, its rivers, its beautiful lakes, and its mountains clothed with green, I have left my sisters in yonder world to dwell among you. Young brave! ask your wise and your great men where I can live and see the happy race continually; ask them what form I shall assume in order to be loved."

Thus discoursed the bright stranger. The young man awoke. On stepping out of his lodge he saw the star yet blazing in its accustomed place.

At early dawn the chief's crier was sent round the camp to call every warrior to the Council Lodge. When they had met, the young warrior related his dream. They concluded that the star that had been seen in the South had fallen in love with mankind, and that it was desirous to do well with them.

The next night five tall, noble-looking adventurous braves were sent to welcome the stranger to earth. They went and presented to it a pipe of peace, filled with sweet scented herbs, and were rejoiced to find that it took it from them. As they returned to the village, the star with expanded wing followed, and hovered over their homes till the dawn of day.

Again it came to the young man in a dream, and desired to know where it should live, and what form it should take.

Places were named. On the top of giant trees, or in

flowers. At length it was told to choose a place itself, and it did so.

At first, it dwelt in the white rose of the mountains; but there it was so buried that it could not be seen. It went to the prairie, but it feared the hoof of the buffalo. It next sought the rocky cliff, but there it was so high, that the children whom it loved most could not see it.

"I know where I shall live," said the bright fugitive, "where I can see the gliding canoe of the race I most admire. Children! yes, they shall be my playmates, and I will kiss their brows when they slumber by the side of the cool lakes. The nations shall love me wherever I am."

These words having been said, she alighted on the waters where she saw herself reflected. The next morning, thousands of white flowers were seen on the surface of the lakes, and the Indians gave them this name—"*Wah-be-gwon-nee*," (White Lily.) "Now," continued the old man, "this star lived in the Southern skies. Its brethren can be seen far off in the cold North, hunting the great bear, whilst its sisters watch here in the East and West.

"Children! when you see the lily on the waters, take it in your hands, and hold it to the skies, that it may be happy on earth, as its two sisters, the morning and the evening stars, are happy in heaven."

While tears fell fast from the eyes of all, the old man laid down and was soon silent in sleep.

Since that, I have often plucked the white lily, and

garlanded it around my head—have dipped it in its watery bed—but never have I seen it without remembering the legend of the descending star.

THE FLOWER HUNT.

BY HARRIET WINSLOW LIST.

THE flowers awoke one sunny day
By a shadowy river far away,
And each shook off the dew drops bright,
And whispered softly its dream of the night.

The harebell that grew on the mountain side
Was the first to ring an alarum wide,
Then looking down on the flowers below
And shaking its bright head to and fro;

The vision it told with a mystic air,
For much of wonder and fear was there,
And its sisters looked up with admiring eyes
For its sweet face mirrored the clear blue skies.

The fairy that slept in its azure bell,
And left it just at the midnight knell,
A warning had breathed with his last adieu,
That chilled the hearts of the flowery crew.

Renew not to-morrow your love and bliss,
Dream not to-night of the butterfly's kiss,
For before another sun shall set,
A fearful foe must be shunned or met.

Then every flower with teardrops hung
Its moving melody sadly sung,
For each had a boding dream to tell,
Which chimed with the peal of the blue harebell.

O the woodland moaned then mournfully,
Like the troubled waves of a wind-swept sea,
And leaf and flower rocked to and fro,
In a tremulous dread of coming woe.

A council of war was held straightway,
But whence the foe no seer could say;
And a strife arose, which was sad to see,
Among flowers that had lived so lovingly.

The thistle lifted its purple crown
And threatened to put all its rivals down,
With spears all pointed and armor bright,
It claimed the lead as its natural right;
But the listeners laughed with republican scorn,
When it boasted of being nobly born.

In idle debate the time flew by
Till the sun in the clouded heavens rode high,
And the flowrets trembled at every sound,
As the rose fraught hours were rolling round.

At length on the hushed and listening air,
A murmur was borne to the tremblers there,
At first like the distant waving of trees,
Then nearer and louder it came on the breeze.

Light laughter peals rung merrily out,
And the echoing hills gave back the shout,
To the flowrets all, ah ! sound of fear,
For they knew too well the hunters were near.

From afar they had scented their delicate game,
And onward with cruel haste they came,
With song and with jest, in girlish sport,
Unmindful of all the death they brought.

Little hunting gear the troop displayed,
Their only weapon, a tiny blade,
And a delicate cord to bind their prey,
Which the wooing winds might lure away.

Each flower shrunk to the darkest place,
Lamenting too late its lovely face,
And vainly tried to subdue or hide
The brilliant hues that were once its pride.

The wild rose caught the first maiden's glance,
And paled at sight of her unsheathed lance;
With remorseless haste the blade she drew
Her eager arm was too fatally true,
The rose's last sigh was unheeded, unheard,
And fluttering it fell like a wounded bird.

Poor, faded thing! 'twas the latest comer,
The last and the loveliest rose of summer;
Its blushing leaves were but just unfurled,
It was loth to leave the lovely world.

The clematis climbed round the nearest tree,
And thought to escape captivity;
Wildly and lovingly it clung,
When the spoiler's grasp all its tendrils wrung.

One effort more its embrace to sever,
It fell, and they parted forever and ever;
Its beautiful blossoms were wreathed in the curls,
And round the hats of the reckless girls.

The humming bird had been whispering low,
To the honeysuckle the long day through;
The bee had courted the clover blossom,
And nestled close to its bounteous bosom;

And the laurel opened its honey cell
To the butterfly it loved so well;
But when danger came, the lovers had flown,
And the flowers were left to die alone.

The water lily had lifted up
On the lake's calm bosom its snowy cup,
And with fearless air it floated there,
For to cross the stream no maiden dare;

They marked its grace with wistful eye,
As its fragrant breath on the air came by,
And the lily laughed low their dismay to see,
And unfolded its petals coquettishly.

Dearly the thistle sold its life,
For the blood of the murderer flowed in the strife,
It cast one dying look around,
And saw all its humble comrades bound,
The proud and the meek were alike laid low,
In the stern democracy of woe.

The blue-eyed grass and the mountain pride,
And the ladies' slipper, lay side by side,
The stately sunflower bled on the sod,
With the buttercup and the golden rod,
And the plebeian dandelion fell
By the same rude hand with the blue harebell.

Their incense no more at the sun's first rays,
Will they offer up to their Author's praise,
No more will they start from their morning dream,
Their toilet to make in the silver stream.

The moon rose sad o'er the desolate scene,
To gaze on the path where the spoiler had been;
The river with mournful song flowed on,
Lamenting the beauty and love that had gone.

The flowers meantime all bound and wayworn,
In the captor's train were triumphantly borne,
But not one survived to reach the place,
Their beauty and odor were destined to grace.

Some perished with grief from their loved ones torn,
Some fainted with fear ere the march was done,
The fairest, the sweetest, the greenwood's pride,
All hung their beautiful heads and died.

FLOWERS, as well as animals, are emblems of characters, because they are really characters—and the influence they exert upon us is of a truly vital and passional character, either by their aromas or their visual harmonies. Delicate and impressible persons feel this very sensibly, and it is only heedlessness or prejudice, and the habit of relying rather on the stereotyped notions that we may have been taught as children, than on our own intuitive consciousness, that disinherit nature of spirit, and her children of an intelligence and sentiment, which once interpreted through the same media of sensation, physiognomy and passional dynamics which we use among ourselves, would wonderfully sweeten, brighten and enrich our daily walks and natural communion. It is a true sentiment of that courtesy which ought to subsist between all the children of the Sun and Earth, which makes us pause reluctantly before the act of violent appropriation, which inspires the Poet to

> "Name all the birds without a gun,
> Love the wild rose, and leave it on its stalk."

They live, they feel, they love! and our relations with them should come under a higher law of communion than that of destructive self-appropriation. It should be the mutual interchange of benefits, and the communion of sentiment, whose material element is the magnetic, nervous or biodic aroma.

Reichenbach's Dynamics throws a flood of light upon these arcana which have hitherto been understood only by the most spiritually sensitive persons. The suggestive experiments recorded in that book open a new and vast field of the highest interest in physiology, hygiene, and all the associations of man with external nature. R. seems to have confined himself chiefly to the influences of mineral or inorganic substances on the impressible. It remains to investigate systematically those of the vegetable and animal world.

I shall quote from Darwin's "*Zoonomia*" some evidences of the vitality, sensation and sentiment of plants, though the biodic influence which they exert, manifests a higher order of powers than we could infer from these mechanical observations.

SECT. XIII.—OF VEGETABLE ANIMATION.

I. Vegetables are irritable, mimosa, dionœa muscipula. Vegetable secretions. Vegetable buds are inferior animals, are liable to greater or less irritability. II. Stamens and pistils of plants, show marks of sensibility. III. Vegetables possess some degree of volition. IV. Motions of plants are associated like those of animals. V. Vegetable structure like that of animals: their anthers and stigmas are living creatures. Male-flowers of Vallisneria. Whether vegetables possess ideas? They have organs of sense as of touch and smell, and ideas of external things.

I. The fibres of the vegetable world, as well as those of the animal, are excitable into a variety of motion by the irritations of external objects. This appears particularly in the mimosa or sensitive plant, whose leaves contract on the slightest injury; the dionæa, which is a native of America, presents us with another curious instance of vegetable irritability; its leaves are armed with spines on their upper edge, and are spread on the ground around the stem; when an insect creeps on any of them in its passage to the flower or seed, the leaf shuts up like a steel rat-trap, and destroys its enemy.

The various secretions of vegetables, as of odor, fruit, gum, resin, wax, honey, seem brought about in the same manner as in the glands of animals; the tasteless moisture of the earth is converted by the hop-plant into a bitter juice, as by the caterpillar in the nut-shell, the sweet kernel is converted into a bitter powder, while the power of absorption in the roots and barks of vegetables is excited into action by the fluids applied to their mouths, as to the lacteals and lymphatics of animals.

2. The individuals of the vegetable world may be considered as inferior or less perfect animals; a tree is a congeries of many living buds, and in this respect resembles the branches of coralline, which are a congeries of a multitude of animals. Each of these buds of a tree has its proper leaves or petals for lungs, produces its viviparous or its oviparous offspring in buds or seeds; has its own roots, which extending down the stem of the tree, are interwoven with the roots of the other buds, and form the bark, which is the only living part of the stem, is annually renewed, and is superinduced upon the former bark, which then dies, and with its stagnated juices gradually hardening into wood, forms the concentric circles, which we see in blocks of timber.

The following circumstances evince the individuality of the buds of trees. First, there are many trees, whose whole internal wood is perished, and yet the branches are vegete and healthy. Secondly, the fibres of the barks and trees are chiefly longitudinal, resembling roots, as is beautifully seen in those prepared barks, that were lately brought from Otaheita. Thirdly, in horizontal wounds of the bark of trees, the fibres of the upper lip are always elongated downwards like the roots, but those of the lower lip do not approach to meet them. Fourthly, if you wrap wet moss round any joint of a vine, or cover it with moist earth, roots will shoot out from it. Fifthly, by the inoculation or engrafting of trees, many fruits are produced from one stem. Sixthly, a new tree is produced from a branch plucked from an old one, and set in the ground. Whence it appears that the buds of deciduous trees are so many annual plants, that the bark is a contexture of the roots of each individual bud; and that the internal wood is of no other use but to support them in the air, and that thus they resemble the animal world in their individuality.

The irritability of plants, like that of animals, appears liable to be increased or decreased by habit; for those trees or shrubs, which are brought from a colder climate to a warmer, put out their leaves and blossoms a fortnight sooner than the indigenous ones.

Professor Kalm, in his travels in New York, observes that the apple trees brought from England blossom a fortnight sooner than the native ones. In our country, the shrubs that are brought a degree or two from the North, are observed to flourish better than those which come from the South. The Siberian barley and cabbage are said to grow larger in this climate than the similar more southern vegetables. And our hoards of roots, as of potatoes and onions, germinate with less heat in spring, after they have been accustomed to the winter's cold, than in autumn after the summer's heat.

II. The stamens and pistils of flowers show evident marks of sensibility, not only from many of the stamens and some pistils approaching towards each other at the season of impregnation, but from many of them closing their petals and calices during the cold part of the day. Others close up their leaves during darkness.

The approach of the anthers in many flowers to the stigmas, and of the pistils of some flowers to the anthers, must be ascribed to the passion of love, and hence belongs to sensation, and not to irritation.

III. That the vegetable world possesses some degree of voluntary powers, appears from the necessity to sleep, which involves the temporary abolition of voluntary power. This voluntary power seems to be exerted in circular movement of the tendrils of vines, and other climbing vegetables; or in the efforts to turn the upper surface of their leaves, or their flowers to the light.

IV. The association of fibrous motions is observable in the vegetable world, as well as in the animal. The divisions of the leaves of the sensitive plant have been accustomed to contract at the same time from the absence of light; hence, if by any other circumstance, as a slight stroke or injury, one division is irritated into contraction, the neighboring ones contract also, from their motions being associated with those of the irritated part. So the various stamina of the class syngenesia have been accustomed to contract together in the evening, and thence if you stimulate one of them with a pin, they all contract from their acquired associations.

To evince that the collapsing of the sensitive plant is not owing to any mechanical vibrations propagated along the whole branch, when a single leaf is struck with the finger; a leaf of it was slit with sharp scissors, and some seconds of time passed before the plant seemed sensible of the injury, and then the whole branch collapsed as far as the principal stem: this experiment was repeated several times with the least possible impulse to the plant.

V. For the numerous circumstances in which vegetable buds are analogous to animals, the reader is referred to the additional notes at the end of the Botanic Garden, Part 1. It is there shown, that the roots of vegetables resemble the lacteal system of animals; the sap-vessels in the early spring, before their leaves expand, are analogous to the placental vessels of the fœtus; that the leaves of land-plants resemble lungs, and those of aquatic plants the gills of fish; that there are other systems of vessels resembling the vena portarum of quadrupeds, or the aorta of fish; that the digestive power of vegetables is similar to that of animals, converting the fluids, which they absorb, into sugar; that their seeds resemble the eggs of animals, and their buds and bulbs their viviparous offspring. And, lastly, that the anthers and stigmas are real animals, attached indeed to their parent tree like the polypi or coral insects, but capable of spontaneous motion; that they are affected with the passion of love, and furnished with powers of reproducing their species, and are fed with honey like the moths and butterflies, which plunder their nectaries. See *Botanic Garden*, Part I. add. note xxxix.

The male flowers of Vallisneria approach still nearer to apparent animality, as they detach themselves from the parent plant, and float on the surface of the water to the female ones.—*Botanic Garden*, Part II. Art. Vallisneria. Other flowers of the classes of monecia and diecia, and polygamia, discharge the fecundating farina, which floating in the air is carried to the stigma of the female flowers, and that at considerable distances. Can this be affected by any specific attraction? or, like the diffusion of the odorous particles of flowers, is it left to the currents of winds, and the accidental miscarriages of it counteracted by the quantity of its production?

This leads us to a curious inquiry, whether vegetables have ideas of external things? As all our ideas are originally received by our senses, the question may be changed to, whether vegetables possess any organs of sense? Certain it is, that they possess a sense of heat and cold, another of moisture and dryness, and another of light and darkness; for they close their petals occasionally from the presence of cold, moisture, or darkness. And it has been already shown, that these actions cannot be performed simply from irritation, because cold and darkness are negative quantities, and on that account sensation or volition are implied, and in consequence a sensorium or union of their nerves. So when we go into the light, we contract the iris; not from any stimulus of the light on the fine muscles of the iris, but from its motions being associated with the sensation of too much light on the retina: which could not take place without a sensorium or centre of union of the nerves of the iris with those of vision. See *Botanic Garden*, Part I, Canto 3. l. 440.

Besides these organs of sense, which distinguish cold, moisture, and darkness, the leaves of mimosa, and of dionæa, and of drosera, and the stamens of many flowers, as of the berberry, and the numerous class of syngenesia, are sensible to mechanic impact, that is, they possess a sense of touch, as well as a common sensorium; by the medium of which their muscles are excited into action. Lastly, in many flowers, the anthers when mature, approach the stigma, in others the female organ approaches to the male. In a plant of collinsonia, a branch of which is now before me, the two yellow stamens are about three-eighths of an inch high, and diverge from each other, at an angle of about fifteen degrees, the purple style is half an inch high, and in some flowers is now applied to the stamen on the right hand, and in others to that of the left, and will, I suppose, change place to-morrow in those where the anthers have not yet effused their powder.

I ask, by what means are the anthers in many flowers, and stigmas in other flowers, directed to find their paramours? How do either of them know, that the other exists in their vicinity? Is this curious kind of storge produced by mechanic attraction, or by the sensation of love? The latter opinion is supported by the strongest analogy, because a reproduction of the species is the consequence; and then another organ of sense must be wanted to direct these vegetable amourettes to find each other, one probably analogous to our sense of smell, which in the animal world directs the new-born infant to its source of nourishment, and they may thus possess a faculty of perceiving as well as of producing odors.

Thus, besides a kind of taste at the extremities of their roots, similar to that of the extremities of our lacteal vessels, for the purpose of selecting their proper food; and besides different kinds of irritability residing in the various glands, which separate honey, wax, resin, and other juices from their blood; vegetable life seems to possess an organ of sense to distinguish the variations of heat, another to distinguish the varying degrees of moisture, another of light, another of touch, and probably another analogous to our sense of smell. To these must be added the indubitable evidence of their passion of love, and I think we may truly conclude, that they are furnished with a common sensorium belonging to each bud, and that they must occasionally repeat those perceptions either in their dreams or waking hours, and consequently possess ideas of so many of the properties of the external world, and of their own existence.

In the department of organic analogy, Homœopathy embraces the most important and practical applications. This principle, that the same medicines cause and cure similar forms of disease, and not such as are opposite, was clearly announced by Hippocrates, and observed by physicians occasionally, in their records of cures, but was first conscientiously made the basis of a regular course of experiment and of therapeutics, by Samuel Hahnemann, in the last century. When experimental exhibition of a certain drug in sufficiently numerous and varied cases, has shown its range of action on the different temperaments, ages and sexes, and a well-digested record or codex of symptoms (which, sooth to say, has never yet been made), allows us to compare the picture of disease which a patient presents, with those artificially induced by drugs on their experimenters; the curative drug may be chosen by the analogy of the symptoms.

Lamentably confused as the natural groups of induced symptoms have been by the false methods of recorders, the characteristics of a few remedies are still discernible, and a great many cures are every day made in this way, though few in comparison to what may be effected when a more perfect pathogenesis allows Homœopathy to justify its claim as exact science.

As an illustration, I subjoin a few cures of my own, by this employment of analogy in medicine :—

In the Fall of 1850 I was consulted by a lady of Aurora, Ia., on account of her health, some of whose derangements I have the discretion not to explain, but which were analogous to those induced by Belladonna, Nux Vomica and Sepia; the first of which drugs was specifically indicated by attacks of headache without sick stomach, nocturnal throbbing with heat of head and general chilliness, obliging her to sit up all night and hold the head—the slightest motion even of the eyes being intolerable. The vertex, temple and eyes were its seats, and it shifted from point to point. The Belladonna which I gave in infinitesimally small doses, promptly and effectually removed this headache, and its attacks diminished in frequency, so much as to indicate the probability of a permanent cure.

After exposure to a bleak wintry North wind in June 1851, I was seized with inflammatory rheumatism of such severity, that I could with great difficulty move my limbs, and an excellent feather bed seemed to bruise me like rough stones. Fever ran high, and my skin remained perfectly dry. In this condition I took part of a drop of the tincture of Arnica mixed with water every hour or two for ten hours; at the end of which, perspiration broke out, and being encouraged by warm coverings, continued profusely for several hours, effectually relieving me. The fever afterwards returned with the muscular paralysis, but a drop of Aconite exhibited in the same way as the Arnica, restored free motion within twelve hours, and radically cured the disease, which has never since shown the slightest symptom of return. Now, any one who will look into Jahr's large Materia Medica or Symptomen Codex, may convince themselves that these drugs were in specific analogy with the disease in question. (See my little Treatise on Homœopathy, published by Radde.)

In concluding this volume on analogies, I venture to suggest a very beautiful application of nature's organic symbolism to the truer adornment of our burial grounds. No monument of stone is so durable as a great tree,—so beautiful, or capable by any inscription of words of such touching significance; for the waving boughs whose shade protects us and whose fruit refreshes, while their serial arborescence teach the sublimest laws of nature, beside the hieroglyphical lessons specific to each kind; appeal to the soul through the charm of the senses, combining the practical with the ideal, wisdom with charm. Our written language can never come home like these primal voices of nature. The costly marble monument, whose elaborate chiselling soon wearies the eye; imprisons the organic elements of the body, refusing them all participation or interflow with nature's tides of life and use in the eternal re-kindling of her fires from their ashes, which the ancients depicted in their fable of the Phœnix. The tree, which costs us only a moment of pleasure to plant it, continues through progressive ages to expand in beneficent uses, and while adding to the sum of natural wealth and enjoyment, it liberates by its absorbent roots, the atoms of the body beneath it, and gives them again to move, to live, to breathe and bloom in other forms, as it returns them to the circuit of natural functions and uses. If the gravestone continues after death the symbol of that passional oppression in which the life of the civilizee has been choked down, the green waving flower and fruit-bearing tree depict the luxuriant spontaneity of the true soul-world, whether in the harmonies of this life or of that beyond the grave.

The species of tree or plant will be determined by the character of the deceased. A man who was a pillar of society will have a pine, a chestnut, or a shell-bark tree planted over his grave,—the graceful woman a locust, acacia or mimosa—the child a jessamine vine, a honeysuckle or azalia: the young virgin a rose-bush; the generous friend a grape-vine; the passional queen an orange tree; the patriarch an oak or an apple tree. All this will be only the next most natural step to the beautiful cemeteries already laid out near our great cities, and the symbolism will be still more charming when employed on private estates throughout our country, now, and afterwards in the associations which will grow up.

The stone is an appurtenance of faithless materialism—the tree of religious intelligence. One suggests *de profundis*, the other adds *resurgam*.

END OF VOL. I.

NOW IN PRESS, OR IN PREPARATION,

BY THE SAME AUTHOR.

THE ZEND-AVESTA AND SOLAR RELIGIONS.

THE SUN HIEROGLYPHIC OF GOD, and Practical Revelations of the Solar Ray.

THE TRINITY AND THE INCARNATION,

LOVE VERSUS MARRIAGE.

PASSIONAL HYGIENE.

HOMŒOPATHY; A Theoretic Demonstration.

INDUSTRIAL ORGANIZATION and **PASSIONAL EQUILIBRIA.** A Translation of the French of Victor Considerant.

THE HUMAN TRINITY, or Three Aspects of Life.

PRACTICAL EDUCATION, or the Development of Natural Vocations.

PASSIONAL ZOOLOGY, or Spirit of Beasts; being a Translation from the French of A. Toussenel.

www.ingramcontent.com/pod-product-compliance
Lightning Source LLC
LaVergne TN
LVHW010240110826
845151LV00004B/1348
9781425524203